Destined

to

Increase

STUDY MANUAL FOR SUCCESS

DARROW SMITH

ISBN 978-1-0980-1691-3 (paperback)
ISBN 978-1-0980-1692-0 (digital)

Christian Faith Publishing, Inc.
832 Park Avenue
Meadville, PA 16335
www.christianfaithpublishing.com

Unless otherwise indicated, all Scripture quotations are taken from the New King James Version of the Bible. Copyright © 1982 by Thomas Nelson, Inc.

The Scripture quotation marked KJV is taken from The King James Version Copyright © 1986 by World Bible Publishers, Inc.

Printed in the United States of America

Contents

Introduction

You were destined to increase in everything you do. When the Lord our God created you, you were blessed. In other words, the Creator was invoking divine favor on your life.

Out of all that He created, you were the only one created in His Image and likeness. You were the sole reason for creating the earth. Just as a mother and father prepares for a baby by getting all the things the baby will need for the first six months or so, our Heavenly Father did the same for you. Everything you needed was already put here for you to grow and to succeed in this life.

The Creator had one child and a host of angels, but he wanted more children so that He would love them, and they would love Him. This is why we were created. God wanted His creations to love Him with a true heart. In this book, the Lord has given me the opportunity to write His words to show you that you were destined to increase. He says, "My people are destroyed for lack of knowledge" (Hosea 4:6). I believe the Lord has equipped His people with everything they need. Today the Lord is speaking to you through this book. "I have blessed you, (to) be "fruitful and multiply; fill the earth and subdue it; have dominion over everything the fish of the sea, over the birds of the air, and over every living thing that moves on the earth" (Gen 1:28).

"God gave man dominion over everything on the earth and created mankind after His likeness." In other words, as the Holy Bible confirms, along with many historical events, mankind has dominion over everything on the earth, but one another. Because we (mankind)

5

were created in His likeness, we should love and honor one another, submitting to one another. We are not to have dominion over one another, even though the husband is the head of the wife, we are not to have dominion over her, and wife you are not to have dominion over your husband either.

Mankind was created above all of God's other creations here on earth, to create and have dominion over the earth. Continuing what the Creator God had started when He created the earth and having supreme dominion, gives glory and honor to Him. The same way God created the earth for you and I is the same way we create our heaven here on earth for ourselves until He calls us home or until He returns back again.

You were born with the Purpose to Increase

In order to understand that you were destined to increase, we must go back to the beginning of God's creation.

Day 1:

> In the beginning God created the heavens and the earth. (2) The earth was without form, and void; and darkness was on the face of the deep. And the Spirit of God was hovering over the face of the waters. (3) Then God **said**, 'Let there be light;" and there was light. (Gen 1:1–3)

We see that in the beginning God created the heavens and the earth. And when we look at Genesis chapter one, we see that He did it by speaking words.

> And God saw the light that it was good; and God divided the light from the darkness. God **called** the light Day, and the darkness He called Night. So the evening and the morning were the first day.
> Then God **said:** Let there be a firmament in the midst of the waters, and let it divide the waters from the waters:

Thus God made the firmament, and divided the waters which were under the firmament from the waters which were above the firmament; and it was so.

And God **called** the firmament Heaven. So the evening and the morning were the second day.

Then God **said**, "let the waters under the heavens be gathered together into one place, and let the dry land appear;" and it was so.

And God **called** the dry land Earth, and the gathering together of the waters He called Seas. And God saw that it was good.

Then God **said**, "Let the earth bring forth grass, the herb that yields seed, and the fruit tree that yields fruit according to its kind, whose seed is in itself, on the earth;" and it was so.

And the earth brought forth grass, the herb that yields seed according to its kind, and the tree that yields fruit, whose seed is in itself according to its kind. And God saw that it was good.

So the evening and the morning were the third day.

Then God **said**, "Let there be lights in the firmament of the heavens to divide the day from the night; and let them be for signs and seasons, and for days and years;

"And let them be for lights in the firmament of the heavens to give light on the earth;" and it was so.

Then God made two great lights: the greater light to rule the day, and the lesser light to rule the night. He made the stars also.

God set them in the firmament of the heavens to give light on the earth.

And to rule over the day and over the night, and to divide the light from the darkness. And God saw that it was good.

So the evening and the morning were the fourth day.

Then God **said**, "Let the waters abound with an abundance of living creatures, and let birds fly above the earth across the face of the firmament of the heavens"

So God created great sea creatures and every living thing that moves, with which the waters abounded, according to their kind, and every winged bird according to its kind. And God saw that it was good.

And God blessed them, saying, "Be fruitful and multiply, and fill the waters in the seas, and let birds multiply on the earth.

So the evening and the morning were the fifth day.

Then God **said**, "Let the earth bring forth the living creature according to its kind: cattle and creeping thing and beast of the earth, each according to its kind;" and it was so.

And God made the beast of the earth according to its kind, cattle according to its kind, and everything that creeps on the earth according to its kind. And God saw that it was good. (Gen. 1: 4–25)

In six days, God spoke everything into existence that His new children would need.

Ten times throughout these twenty-five verses, you see where God either called things into existence or spoke them into existence. The number ten is regarded as the most perfect of numbers, and before he made man, ten times God used words to prepare for His creation of mankind.

Day 1, God created light. Day 2, God separated the waters in heaven from the waters on earth. Day 3, God created plant life. Day 4, God created the sun, moon, and stars (to give light to the earth) amazing, Day 5, God created fish and fowl. Day 6, God created land creatures and mankind, and on the seventh day, God rested.

Day 6, mankind was created and blessed to increase on the earth. In other words, mankind was destined to increase! The word, "destined," means to predetermine.[1]

"Increase" means to become greater in size, amount, degree, etc.[2]

Replenish means to fill up, be full; to be ordained; fulfilled.[3]

Have you ever wondered why ever since you were a baby, you wanted to increase? You wanted to crawl, then walk, and soon after, you wanted to run. You wanted to get married, have children, buy a car, and so on. All your life, you have wanted to increase, to get taller, get more money—in whatever we are doing by nature, we wanted to increase. And that comes from the command God spoke over mankind's life to be fruitful (increase), replenish (fill up) the earth with things (people, houses, cars, buildings, and churches, etc.). Now when we give up, and do not want to increase, the enemy has convinced you of something other than what God spoke over our lives (be fruitful, multiply, and replenish the earth). Some areas where the enemy attacks are sickness, depression, lack, fear, and low self-esteem. These are all devices of the enemy to keep mankind from increasing.

> Then God **said,** "Let Us make man in our image, according to our likeness: let them have dominion over the fish of the sea, over the birds of the air, and over the cattle, over all the earth and over every creeping thing that creeps on the earth.

---

[1] Charlton Laird, *Websters New World Thesaurus* (New York, NY: Warner Books, 1983).
[2] Ibid.
[3] Ibid.

"So God created man in His own image; in the image of God He created him; male and female He created them.

Then God blessed them, and God **said** to them. "Be fruitful and multiply; fill the earth and subdue it; have dominion over the fish of the sea, over the birds of the air, and over every living thing that moves on the earth.

And God **said**, "See, I have given you every herb that yields seed which is on the face of all the earth, and every tree whose fruit yields seed; to you it shall be for food.

Also, to every beast of the earth, to every bird of the air, and to everything that creeps on the earth, in which there is life, I have given every green herb for food;" and it was so.

Then God saw everything that He had made, and indeed it was very good. So the evening and the morning were the sixth day." (Gen 1:26–31)

God created male and female both in His own image and likeness to be blessed, to increase, multiply and fill the earth with things. This was a command spoken by The Creator God to bring glory to Him and would fulfill His children's desires.

You were created In the Likeness of God

After everything was created, God said, "Let Us make man in our image according to our likeness, and it was so. Mankind was the only creation created in the image and likeness of our Creator" (v. 26). Readers, we are created in the image and likeness of our creator, and we have His likeness. What are some of His characteristics that we have in us? We have the Ability to "call those things which do not exist as though they did." Romans 4:17c says it this way, "And called those things which be not as though they were."

You too were destined to call things that be not as though they were. Why? Because you are created in the image and likeness of Almighty God the Creator. You have the ability to create your own environment with your words. Words are powerful. With words, you may encourage a person or curse them. With words, you may tear down or build up, and with words, you may create or destroy. In a corporation, the most powerful person in the company is the president or CEO. The person who gives the word on a matter has the authority just as a person who tells others what to do has authority. It's not the strong laborer who uses physical labor who has authority but the person who gives the orders by speaking words has the authority. The words of a president of a country will affect the whole country; the words that you speak about yourself will affect your whole life.

In the New Testament, the centurion understood this principle:

> "Now when Jesus had entered Capernaum, a centurion came to Him, pleading with Him. Saying; Lord, my servant is lying at home paralyzed, dreadfully tormented." And Jesus said to him, "I will come and heal him." The centurion answered and said, "Lord, I am not worthy that you should come under my roof. But only speak a word, and my servant will be healed. "For I also am a man under authority, having soldiers under me. And I say to this one, 'Go,' and he goes; and to another, 'Come,' and he comes; and to my servant, 'Do this,' and he does it." (Matt. 8:5–9)

Authority is exercised by a word and carried out by a word. A father and mother instruct their children with words. A manager gives assignments with words.

From the beginning of time, we see that the power and authority is in our mouth. The first assignment God the Creator gave mankind was to use his authority, which is to speak. Look at Genesis 2:19, "Out of the ground the Lord God formed every beast of the field and every bird of the air, and brought them to Adam to see what he would call them. And whatever Adam called each living creature that was its name."

Mankind's very first assignment was to use his God-given ability to speak a word and have it come to pass. (*Whatever Adam called each living creature that was its name*). Just as the heavenly Father did at creation, so does mankind because we were created in His image and likeness. Whatever comes your way, you have the ability to name it. You may change your situations good or bad by what you call it. If you call it blessed than it is blessed, if you call yourself healed, then you are healed. The power is in your mouth to succeed or to fail here on the earth.

Adam and Eve had the power to withstand the serpent in Genesis chapter three. Rather than repeat and stand on the words of God, they went along with the words of the serpent. The serpent talks to the soul of man, whereas God speaks to the spirit of man. The two, spirit and soul, are so closely related because both God breathed into spiritual existence within the human body. The only thing that may separate them is the word of God. Hebrew 4:12 says, "For the Word of God is quick, and powerful, and sharper than any two-edge sword, piercing even to the dividing asunder of soul and spirit."

Spirit is defined as a non-material being that influences that part that is the Nature of God. God is a Spirit.

Soul is defined as the moral or emotional nature of a person, feelings, and the thinking.

Now in this next passage, the serpent speaks to their soul.

> Now the serpent was more cunning than any beast of the field which the Lord God had made. And he said to the woman, Has God indeed said, "You shall not eat of every tree of the garden?"
>
> And the woman said to the serpent, "We may eat the fruit of the trees of the garden;
>
> But of the fruit of the tree which is in the midst of the garden, God has said, "You shall not eat it, nor shall you touch it, lest you die."
>
> Then the serpent said to the woman, "You will not surely die,
>
> For God knows that in the day you eat of it your eyes will be opened, and you will be like God, knowing good and evil.
>
> So when the woman saw that the tree was good for food, that it was pleasant to the eyes, and a tree desirable to make one wise, she took of its fruit and ate. She also gave to her husband with her, and he ate. (Gen. 3:1–6)

The serpent said to the woman "you will not die." God said, "She would die." With these cunning words from the serpent, the woman began to look at the fruit to see it was desirable to herself (soul or flesh). So she and her husband disobeyed the Lord God and did eat of the tree, causing both of them to sin against God's Word.

> Death and life are in the power of the tongue, and those who love it will eat its fruit. (Prov. 18:21)

So, whether you speak positive (good) words or negative (bad) words, the power lies in our tongue. However, God intends for mankind to desire the good things of the earth and speak the good into existence. He created and gave you your mouth to create things for your good and fill the earth with material things (clothes, houses, transportation, TV's, phones, computers, etc). However, God set some ground rules to keep us in His will, and if we will adhere to His words, we will live by them and not die (spiritually). Seeking His Word and doing things His way, we will increase as He said we would. God is not forcing increase on mankind. It is His desire that mankind would increase. Mankind was created to be free moral agents that may make their own choices, though God would have mankind to choose Him and His ways over the serpent (devil, Satan, great dragon) ways. Adam and Eve chose what looked good or what appeared would make one wise (fleshly desires), and apparently, they did not hold on in their spirits nor the words of the Lord, to obey when God said they would surely die if they ate of the tree of good and evil.

When mankind chose to disobey God, they were acting on their flesh (natural feelings), which is the part of mankind that is subject to temptation by the enemy's tricks. The enemy I'm speaking of is the devil, God's enemy since the beginning of earth's creation. I have been calling God's creation of man as mankind. However, what God wants are more children. The Lord Jesus was the first and only begotten Son of God until the rebirth of mankind. At the rebirth, which is referred to as being born again, one is adopted into the family of God and then reassured that they are now children of God. In John 3:3, and 5, "Verily, verily, I say unto thee, except a man be born again, he cannot see the kingdom of God", and in verse five "Jesus answered, "Verily, verily, I say unto thee, except a man be born of water and of the Spirit, he cannot enter into the kingdom of God." Also, in Romans 8:14–17a, "For as many as are led by the Spirit of God, they are the sons of God. For ye have not received the spirit of bondage again to fear; but ye have received the Spirit of adoption, whereby we cry, Abba, Father. The Spirit itself beareth witness with our spirit, that we are the children of God; and if children, then heirs; heirs of God, and joint-heirs; with Christ."

And to be born again, God sent His only begotten Son, Jesus into the world to die for the sins of the world, and on the third day after He had been dead in a tomb, God raised Jesus up from the dead. Now, some forty days after His rise up from the dead, He was seen walking on the earth by many witnesses. Then God called Him up to heaven and seated Him on His right hand, giving the Lord Jesus all power in heaven and on the earth. Anyone who believes this act of God by confessing this belief and confesses his or her sins and ask for forgiveness. This act of the believer represents the spirit part of the rebirth and the baptism in the Lord Jesus's name is the water part of the new rebirth. This person is now born again into the family of God and is now a child of God, an heir and joint heir with "the Christ." The Holy Bible says, "Marvel not that I said unto thee, ye must be born again" (John 3:7). You must be born again to be His child. Amen!

Man was made to reign forever in the earth without dying. God said if you eat of the tree of good and evil, you will surely die. Keep in mind a thousand years is like a day to the Lord. Adam lived to be 930 years, less than a day to God.

> For a thousand years in your sight are like yesterday when it is past, and like a watch in the night. (Ps. 90:4)

According to scripture, Adam and Eve who were to live forever only lived within a day in the eyes of the Creator.

The Lord our God is not so concerned about time since God is the beginning and the end. God was from the beginning because He created the beginning.

God created man in His image and his likeness. Genesis 1:1–3 says, "The beginning God created the heaven and the earth. 2. And the earth was without form, and void; and darkness was upon the face of the deep. And the spirit of God moved upon the face of the waters. And God said, "Let there be light: and there was light."

When the word, "God," is used here, it is in Hebrew, Elohim (plural), meaning more than one. We see the Holy Spirit in verse 2, we see the Word (God said) in verse 3, and God the Father is the mastermind behind the Godhead. Together, they form the Godhead or the Trinity, the three in one. New Testament speaks of the Godhead. 1 John 5:7 says, "For there are three that bear witness in heaven: the Father, the Word, and the Holy Spirit; and these three are one."

And the three are in agreement on everything. Three represents the number of completion. Just think about it, if Jesus had said, "No, father, I will not go to the cross," where would we be, or if the Holy Spirit said, "I will not go down to those rebellious people." Instead the Godhead was in total agreement with one another, God the Father gave the vision, God the Son carried it out, and the Holy Spirit provided the Power and means to do it. Glory to God. The Bible says, "Every word will be established by two or three witnesses." (Matt 18:16). This means that if you just had two witnesses you may still get it done. However, to be in God's perfect will, you would need three witnesses, three being the number of completion.

You were created in the image of God—soul, body, and spirit. Yes, you are three in one. Your spirit and soul are the real you just as God is a spirit. Your body is your house for your spirit, Jesus was the word made flesh (body). And your soul (thoughts, emotions, feelings) is the decision maker as with God the Father the head and the decision maker. The three in one! In order to operate in the image of God, the three must line up in agreement. Adam and Eve were created complete, but in the garden account, a spiritual separation from God took place. You see what connects mankind to the Lord our God is our spirits. John 4:23–24 says, "God is Spirit, and those who worship Him must worship in spirit and truth. But the hour is coming, and now is, when the true worshipers will worship the Father in spirit and truth; for the Father is seeking such to worship Him."

So many people are looking to be complete, but in all the wrong ways. Some think it's having a lot of money that will complete them, they soon find out different. Many stars and athletes are finding out, money, things, and power is not the answer for completeness. Only being connected to God will complete you. God will feed your spirit through His word, your spirit will then nourish your soul and your soul notifies your body what to do. Then and only then may mankind be complete, full, whole and at peace.

The apostle Paul refers it as to be "led by the Spirit, and you will not fulfill the lust of the flesh" (Gal 5:16–26).

God, who sees all, knows all and who knows the beginning from the end, had a backup plan to redeem man back to his complete state through the blood of Jesus. You may have whatever you say, and it only takes two witnesses, your soul and your body. Adam and Eve showed us this. Their souls were in agreement with the decision to eat of the tree of knowledge this is why they felt the way they did condemned and hiding themselves from God afterwards. A separation took place. They were no longer in right standing with their Creator, but they did get what they spoke out of their mouth because the soul and the body were in agreement. But since the spirit was left out, it wasn't the will of God, but the will of their soul's desires.

The spirit did not move the children of Babel, whom we will discuss later, because they wanted to make a name for themselves, and the spirit of God was not in it. Because their souls agreed with their body (mouth, and bodily actions), they got what they wanted, until God said hey, I must stop them, seeing that it's not my will for them. Genesis 11:6–9 says, "And the Lord said, "Indeed the people are one and they all have one language, and this is what they begin to do; now nothing that they propose to do will be withheld from them. Come, let Us go down and there confuse their language, that they may not understand one another's speech. So the Lord scattered them abroad from there over the face of all the earth, and they ceased building the city. Therefore, its name is called Babel, because there the Lord confused the language of all the earth; and from there the Lord scattered them abroad over the face of all the earth."

They were unable to understand one another anymore, therefore causing them not to be in agreement and scattered them throughout the world from that point.

You wonder why sinners say things and it comes to pass? It is because they have two witnesses within themselves, soul and body. It only takes two of the three to agree. But the only way that the Lord God is involved in it is for all three to agree (spirit, soul, and body).

I had a friend that would go to the gambling boat, he'd believe and confess that he would win, and that is what would happen. It wasn't until he started to doubt if he would continue to win that he began to lose. You see, you can have what you want when you believe and speak, but the question remains, is it the will of God for your life? When you desire the will of God, He will give you your desires, which will be in line with His will for your life, and you will be complete in Him. I would rather be in the will of God then to have all the money in the world. Money cannot bring you fulfillment or happiness, but through the Lord Jesus, we may have the abundant life and eternal life to come. And to be complete is to have all three of your makeup in line. Your spirit, soul, and your body must be in agreement as with what the Father, Son, and the Holy Spirit are in agreement, and in His perfect will.

Joseph and Abraham were in the Creator's perfect will, even though one was sold and the other called into a famine. The outcome of God still prevailed. God will usually give us the beginning and the end, but we must walk by faith in the between times and if we are "led by the Spirit of God, all things will work out for our good" (Rom. 8:28). Amen!

The Godhead made you so who better would know what is best for you, the serpent or God? It's like buying a CD from the manufacture, getting the highest quality, or buying one from a bootleg (copier, illegal distributor) poor quality. It may be cheaper and easier to buy from a bootlegger, but the quality and the longevity are not there. Only the maker of a thing will understand its true value and what it was designed to be, and that is God the Creator.

You must be Born Again

God had a plan to get man back into his original state (spirit, soul and body). This plan was to be complete as the Godhead is complete and in total agreement. After the fall of mankind, we all were born into sin, making them incomplete (soul and body only), the spirit part is dead until the new rebirth takes place. This tragedy only occurred because of the sin of Adam and Eve back in the Garden of Eden when they both disobeyed God and ate of the tree of knowledge of good and evil. From that time until now, all are born into sin. As you have probably noticed, sin would grow worst, and mankind would inherit the nature and characteristics of their ancestors, going all the way back to Adam and Eve. So God had to do something drastic, send His only begotten Son (Jesus) into the world to die for the sins of the world. This allowed mankind to be born again in the Spirit if they believed on Him (Son) and He who sent the son (God).

Remember, the spirit is that part of man that is connected with God. This time, God would be more merciful, and He would send His only begotten Son the Lord Jesus to show the way.

In order to be complete and in the perfect Will of God, you must first be born again. "Jesus answered and said to him." "Most assuredly, I say to you, unless one is born again, he cannot see the kingdom of God." Nicodemus said to Him, "How can a man be born when he is old? Can he enter a second time into his mother's womb and be born?" Jesus answered, "Most assuredly, I say

> to you, unless one is born of water and the Spirit, he cannot enter the kingdom of God. "That which is born of the flesh is flesh, and that which is born of the Spirit is spirit. (John 3:3–6)
>
> I am the door, If anyone enters by Me, he will be saved, and will go in and out and find pasture. "The thief does not come except to steal, and to kill, and to destroy, I have come that they may have life, and that they may have it more abundantly. (John 10:9–10)
>
> Jesus said to him, "I am the way, the truth, and the life, No one comes to the Father except through me. (John 14:6)

Later I will explain more on this matter, to be born of the Spirit is to confess with your mouth the Lord Jesus and, "Believe in your heart that God has raised Him from the dead, you will be saved" (Rom. 10:9).

> And to be born of the water is to be baptized, or do you not know that as many of us as were baptized into Christ Jesus were baptized into His death? Therefore we were buried with Him through baptism into death, and just as Christ was raised from the dead by the glory of the Father, even so we also should walk in newness of life. For if we have been united together in the likeness of His death, certainly we also shall be in the likeness of His resurrection. Knowing this, that our old man was crucified with Him that the body of sin might be done away with that we should no longer be slaves of sin. For he who has died has been freed from sin. Now if we died with Christ, we believe that we shall also live with Him. (Rom. 6:3–8).

We become children of the Most High God and joint heirs with the Son Jesus (Rom. 8:16–17). We are not just God's creation, but now we are the children of God. "Abraham was a friend of God" (James 2:23), but we are God's children through the rebirth. Children are entitled to more privileges. We may say "Abba Father" and He will love you more than your natural fathers could ever love us. The gold is His; the Silver is His, our God created everything that is created. And just as a loving father would, He wants to give it to you. Even though the enemy tries to "steal from God's children, kill God's children, and destroy God's children," God still destined His Children to increase in all that they do. Now, all your past has been forgiven, and your spirit has been reconciled to God your Father, you are complete in Him.

Therefore, if anyone is in Christ, he is a new creation; old things have passed away; behold, all things have become new. Now all things are of God, who has reconciled us to Himself through Jesus Christ, and has given us the ministry of reconciliation. That is, that God was in Christ reconciling the world to Himself, not imputing their trespasses to them, and has committed to us the word of reconciliation. Now then, we are ambassadors for Christ, as though God were pleading through us: we implore you on Christ's behalf, be reconciled to God. For He made Him who knew no sin to be sin for us, that we might become the righteousness of God in Him. (2 Cor. 5:17–21)

The Spirit Himself bears witness with our spirit that we are children of God. 17. And if children, then heirs—heirs of God and joint heirs with Christ, if indeed we suffer with Him, that we may also be glorified together. (Rom. 8:16–17)

After one is born again. they have now become children of God. Remember from earlier in the book, to be born of "water and of the spirit, one must be born again" This entitle you to 1 John 5:4, which says, "For whosoever is born of God overcometh the world: and this is the victory that overcometh the world, even our faith." That means you have the victory over everything that comes against you in the world. No mountain may stand in your way, no crisis may bring you completely down, no trouble will last always, and nothing may stand against you as a child of God. Scriptures say, "What shall we then say to these things? If God be for us who can be against us" (Rom. 8:31).

When we seek to do God's will, we have all of heaven on our side backing us up. Angels are being dispersed for us every time we pray in the Name of the Lord Jesus. In many words, the Bible references God's children as living by faith in a faithful God who cannot lie. Especially now, in order to receive this word from God, you must receive it by faith, taking to account every scripture that this book outlines. You must believe the Word of God in order to receive the things of God. The Holy Bible uncovers the fact that you were destined to increase (be fruitful, multiply, replenish the earth). You were created in His Image and likeness and given dominion over all the earth. You must also believe God loves you and will forgive you of your sins, when you repent of your sins. "If we confess our sins, he (God) is faithful and just to forgive us our sins, and to cleanse us from all unrighteousness" (1 John 1:9). Once we have been cleansed of unrighteousness, it makes us righteous again in His sight, as simple as that.

The benefits of being Born Again

If you are born again or ready to be born again at that point, you are a child of the Most High God. Glory to God! To be a child of God is bigger than anything else that one would ever imagine being. It's better than being the child of Bill Gates or Oprah Winfrey, two of the riches people in the U.S, for God created them too. And as His child, the Lord Jesus, in whom we are joint heirs with will supply your needs and answer your prayers. The Lord God says, "And whatsoever ye shall ask in my name, that will I do, that the Father may be glorified in the Son. If ye shall ask any thing in my name, I will do it" (John 14:13–14).

Now to be born again completes the three in one man, (body, soul, spirit, old things are passed away) but it does not erase your memory. What I mean is yes now all our sins are forgiven, and we have been restored back into our rightful place, but our soul (mind, thinking), still remembers the old you. So we must now renew our minds (soul). Your soul feeds off of what it sees, hears, or feels. And your spirit feeds off the Word and Spirit of God. So if you feed your spirit, your spirit in return will feed your soul, and your soul will direct your body. All three are working as one in agreement with one another.

> And be renewed in the spirit of your mind, and that you put on the new man which was created according to God, in true righteousness and holiness. (Eph. 4:23)

> I beseech you therefore, brethren, by the mercies of God, that you present your bodies a living sacrifice, holy, acceptable to God, which is your reasonable service. 2.And do not be conformed to this world, but be transformed by the renewing of your mind, that you may prove what is that good and *acceptable and perfect will of God* (italics added). (Rom. 12:1–2)

Now your mind is like a computer that stores information. So the memories are still there, but you may or may not use it. When you get new information in your computer memory, you will begin to use it. And if the old memory pops up one day, use your mouse (in your case, your mouth) to delete it and tell it to go back where it came from. The Holy Spirit will reveal the tricks of the enemy to you. Your response is to rebuke it, keep in mind you may have whatever you believe and speak. The Spirit will lead you, so be mindful for His leading you. Then you believe what you received from the Spirit to cast it down, and then you speak it out. Keep your new man clean from the things of the enemy. Make your house (body) clean and complete by doing the will of your God, by repenting of things you may do wrong, and asking for forgiveness when needed.

The Lord Jesus gives an example of mixing the new with the old in Matthew with the analogy of the new wineskins.

> Nor do they put new wine into old wineskins, or else the wineskins break, the wine is spilled, and the wineskins are ruined. But they put new wine into new wineskins, and both are preserved. (Matt. 9:17)

You have a new spirit after your Heavenly Father's own kind. When you repent of your sins and iniquities, your body has now become clean again, and God would have you to be righteous (complete, whole) in Him. Jesus's main purpose was to give us the abundant life. He wanted to make us whole and complete, that is why He went around doing good teaching and preaching the gospel. Casting out demons, feeding the poor, and healing all that were oppressed with something. The Lord Jesus came to make the body whole in order to receive all that God has in store for you. The word, "shalom," is a Hebrew word that means: from the Strong's Concordance 7965, a word in the New King James version is completeness, wholeness, health, peace, welfare, safety, soundness, tranquility, prosperity, perfectness, fullness, rest, harmony, and the absence of agitation or discord. Shalom comes from the root verb *shalom*, meaning to be complete, perfect, and full.

> The Son of God is completely perfect in all things. (Isa. 9:6)

> The Lord bless you and keep you, The Lord make His face shine upon you and be gracious to you. The Lord lift up His face upon you and give you shalom. In the Name of SAR SHALOM— The Prince of Peace.[4] (Num. 6:24–26)

> The Holy Bible says, "The only thing Jesus is coming back for is a glorious church, not having spot or wrinkle or any such thing, but that she should be holy and without" (Eph. 5:27).

> Now may the God of peace Himself sanctify you completely; and may your whole spirit, soul, and body be preserved blameless at the coming of our Lord Jesus Christ. (1 Thess. 5:23)

> The word of God is living and powerful, and sharper than any two-edged sword, piercing even to the division of soul and spirit, and of joints and

---

[4] "David Silver Borrowed from Out of Zion Ministry" http://www.theirfinersfire.org/meaning_of _shalom.htm.

marrow (body) and is a discerner of the thoughts and intents of the heart. (Heb. 4:12)

Let it be the hidden person of the heart (spirit), with the incorruptible beauty of a gentle and quiet spirit, which is very precious in the sight of God. (1 Peter 3:4)

And once you are born again, you inherit the things of God, but the way you receive them is in His word, which is your road map to success. Now that you know who you are, "a child of God," find out what you should do and how you excess the inheritance of God.

For whatever is born of God overcomes the world. And this is the victory that has overcome the world our faith. Who is he who overcomes the world, but he who believes that Jesus is the Son of God? This is He who came by water and blood-Jesus Christ; not only by water, but by water and blood. And it is the Spirit who bears witness, because the Spirit is truth. (1 John 5:4–6)

Now this is the confidence that we have in Him, that if we ask anything according to His will, He hears us, And if we know that He hears us, whatever we ask, we know that we have the petitions that we have asked of Him. (1 John 5:14–15)

No weapon formed against you shall prosper, and every tongue which rises against you in judgment you shall condemn. This is the heritage of the servants of the Lord. And their righteousness is from Me," Says the Lord. (Isa. 54:17)

Child of God, claim your inheritance. Find out in the word of God (Holy Bible) how to live right and stay a faithful child of your Heavenly Father (God). Keep busy doing kingdom work, for He has given us the ministry of reconciliation (leading others to Him). Not to keep His love and forgiveness to yourself, but to go out and share it with the world, and while you are doing His business, He will make sure your needs are taking care of (2 Cor. 5:18; Mark 16:15; Acts 1:8). There are no limits on what you may do, or have, when you are "walking in the spirit" (Gal 5:16). You were destined to increase! Stand on these words, you were destined to Increase! To increase spiritually, physically and financially, all for His glory in the name of the Lord Jesus. Yes, you were destined to Increase!

And when you are increasing in the things of God the kingdom of God is being increased. When you share the ministry of reconciliation (the good news that we may be reconciled back to God), then will mankind multiply after the image and likeness of "the Creator God."

So we were destined from the beginning to be like our Creator. Our Creator spoke when He wanted something done. He creates things into existence by speaking. You have the same ability in you. Day sixth, you were commanded to be fruitful (flourish, increase, bring forth, grow) multiply (to increase in number, to gain after its kind), and replenish (fill up, be full).

The very first word God said to mankind was to be fruitful (increase) (Gen. 1:28). What we have read in Genesis 1 is God creating everything for man's availability to increase (Gen. 1:29) God said, "I have given you every herb that yields seed." God planted seed in the ground with His Words for plants, trees, and vegetation to grow, to increase and to multiply after their kind. This is a lesson on seedtime and harvest. God made seed to grow for increase. God did not create the grass, but seed for grass to grow in the beginning. God likes to see increase. Jesus could have appeared on earth like Melchizedek, but I believe God wanted to watch His Son, Jesus, grow—as does He wants to see mankind grow and flourish spiritually, physically, and financially.

The Lord God <u>planted a garden</u> eastward in Eden, and there He put the man whom He had formed… <u>And out of the ground</u> the Lord God made every tree grow that is pleasant to the sight and good for food. The tree of life was also in the midst of the garden, and the tree of the knowledge of good and evil. (Gen. 2:8–9)

God created seed to grow and on the seventh day God rested. God rested and looked on His work of increase. Everything God made came from the earth. For years, scientists argued that it was impossible for man or everything on earth to come from the dirt. Through the makeup of DNA, proof has been established that all of mankind makeup has definitely come from the soil of the earth. Though the earth is made of dirt, everything was destined to come from the earth to increase the earth. Through seeds increase would come, seed for plants, seed for trees, seed for animals, and seed (sperm cells) for humans to increase on the earth. Thus, God has given man everything in the earth that They would need to increase the things on the earth. God put gold, silver, metals, minerals, and Irons, here with the soil of the earth to supply the substance needed to increase the earth. Thus, came houses, cars, planes, trains and more things from the earth.

This is the first principle of life that we see throughout creation. Seedtime and Harvest, "While the earth remains, Seedtime and Harvest, Cold and heat, winter and summer, and day and night shall not cease" (Gen. 8:22).

Seedtime and Harvest

The words that you speak are seeds, and like any other seed, it will produce a harvest. In order for a seed to grow, it must be alive and be cared for. A seed requires three fundamental conditions.

> Three fundamental conditions must exist before germination can occur. (1) The embryo must be alive, called seed viability. (2) Any dormancy requirements that prevent germination must be overcome. (3) The proper environmental conditions must exist for germination. Environmental conditions effecting seed germination include; water, oxygen, temperature and light.[5]

The words that we speak are referred to as seed. The Bible lets you know that you shall have whatsoever you desire when you pray (speak).

> Therefore I say to you, whatever things you ask when you pray, believe that you receive them, and you will have them. (Mark 11:24)

---

5 "Seed Dormancy," Wikipedia, April 27, 2019, https://en.wikipedia.org/wiki/Seed_dormancy.

As natural seeds require the right environment conditions, so does the Word sown by mankind. Jesus is speaking in Mark 11:24, "Therefore I **say** (authority given to everyone that hears these words), whatever things you **ask** (speak) when you **pray** (speak), **believe** that you receive them, and you will have them."

When you speak, you are sowing seed. The environment is the condition that you are in, belief or unbelief, now when you believe what you are saying you are continuing to water it with faith (water). The seed (word) is alive. You spoke it, so now it is sown. The next step is to keep the word watered with faith. Faith is your spiritual water. How do we get this spiritual water? Spiritual things require spiritual knowledge, so again we will look in the word of God. Before we do, I ask you this question, are you able to see your words when you speak? Of course not; however, we do see the results of our words. So then we will use spiritual water (faith) that we cannot see, for seed (words) that we cannot see. Now that we understand that our words represent seed, and in order for it to grow into what we say, it will need water (faith) in order to grow. You are probably asking how then do we get the spiritual water (faith).

So then faith comes by hearing, and hearing
by the word of God. (Rom. 10:17)

For those that believe in the word of God and read or hear the word of God, this is your spiritual water. In order to grow, a seed must be watered. Your words need faith in order to grow. Hearing the word of God builds your confidence that God is not only able, but is "willing to do exceeding abundantly above all that we ask or think" (Eph. 3:20). According to the power that works in us, which is the Holy Spirit, once we invite the Lord Jesus into our life, we have the right environment to cause our seed to grow and live a purposed filled life in Christ Jesus. Whose sole purpose was to give us life here in abundance and eternal life to come? Look at John 10:10b, "I (Jesus speaking) have come that they may have life, and that they might have it more abundantly." It's up to you to want the abundant life, that's why He said, "might have." It's a choice, either we want it and believe it will happen, or we don't believe and are afraid to have it. And John 3:16 says, "For God so loved the world that He gave His only begotten Son, that whoever believes in Him should not perish but have everlasting life." The Lord God intended that you have an abundant life now and an everlasting life to come, glory to God.

The Lord Jesus has given His life for anyone that believes that God sent Him here and that Jesus died and rose from the dead by this act alone we are saved. We are reassured that the power is in your tongue, and now you have the Holy Ghost to guide us on how to use it in the manner in which the Creator intended it to be used. Who better than the maker of something to know the most effective way for it to be used? The Heavenly Father has left a blueprint (Holy Bible) to tell you who you are and how to be all you were created to be.

If something is of value, it will be accompanied by instructions. When you purchase an automobile, it comes with instruction—VCR, TV, and even a house comes with instructions. So why wouldn't God's greatest creations come with instructions? Instructions are designed to fully understand and properly use what you have. The same holds true to God's children. Your Heavenly Father, "God the Creator" Inspired the Holy Bible to be written for His Instructions to be left for all mankind to read.

The Sower sows the Word

The Lord Jesus was teaching on the subject of the Word being a seed, and He gave them a parable (short, simple story teaching a moral lesson)[6] of a sower that went out to sow.

> Listen! Behold, a sower went out to sow. "And it happened, as he sowed, that some seed fell by the wayside; and the birds of the air came and devoured it. "Some fell on stony ground, where it did not have much earth; and immediately it sprang up because it had no depth away. "And some seed fell among thorns; and the thorns grew up and choked it, and it yielded no crop. But other seed fell on good ground and yielded a crop that sprang up, increased and produced: come thirtyfold, some sixty, and some a hundred." And He said to them, He who has ears to hear, let him hear!" But when He was alone, those around Him with the twelve asked Him about the parable. And He said to them, "To you it has been given to know the mystery of the kingdom of God; but to those who are outside, all things come in parables, "so that seeing they may see and not perceive, and hearing they may hear and not understand; lest they should turn,

---

[6] Ibid

and their sins be forgiven them.'" And He said to them, "Do you not understand this parable? How then will you understand all the parables? "The sower sows the word. "And these are the ones by the wayside where the word is sown. When they hear, Satan comes immediately and takes away the word that was sown in their hearts. "These likewise are the ones sown an stony ground who, when they hear the word, immediately receive it with gladness; "and they have no root in themselves, and so endure only for a time. Afterward, when tribulation or persecution arises for the word's sake, immediately they stumble. "Now these are the ones sown among thorns; they are the ones who hear the word, "And the cares of this world, the deceitfulness of riches, and the desires for other things entering in choke the word, and it becomes unfruitful. "But these are the ones sown on good ground, those who hear the word, accept it, and bear fruit: some thirtyfold, some sixty, and some a hundred. (Mark 4:3–20)

In verse 20 is where you want to be—when you hear the Word or speak the Word, and you should accept that Word. You then continue to water that word with faith so that the foundation will be strong, and no matter what distractions come up or situations may arise, you will be grounded, knowing that as long as you keep your faith, you will have what you say. When a gardener sows an apple seed, they are expecting for an apple tree to grow. They will not go and dig it up the next day because they don't see anything. They will not dig it up next week if they do not see anything. If it rains hard, or a strong wind would come, the gardener will still not dig the seed back up. The gardener understands that as long as he waters it and cares for it, the seed will produce a harvest.

So many people dig up their seeds with unbelief and doubt, and then wonder why the Bible isn't working for them. No, you must believe that you already have it when you Pray. The devil would use any method to steal your breakthrough. Scriptures says, "The thief does not come except to steal, and to kill, and destroy (John 10:10).

When you realize that the thief is trying to steal from you, you protect yourself with the only weapon that may defeat him and that is the Word of God. Hebrews 4:12 describes the word as being "sharp and powerful." Also, in Ephesians 6:17 the Word is said to be the "sword of the Spirit," and we just read in the book of Mark, The Lord Jesus called the Word, seed. There isn't anything more powerful than your words. Matthew records the word as what justifies a man. Matthew 12:35–37 says, "A good man out of the good treasure of his heart bring forth good things, and an evil man out of the evil treasure brings forth evil things. But I say to you that for every idle word men may speak, they will give account of it in the day of judgement. For by your words you will be justified, and by your words you will be condemned."

Every word you say will produce an outcome. If you say bad things, bad things will happen. If you are always worried about something bad happening, those are seeds that will produce what you are thinking and saying. Examples: if you say I will never get a good deal, you will never get good deal. If you say my marriage is strong and you water those words with faith, you will get it if you leave it planting and do not dig it up. Wait, be patient on your seed and allow it to grow into this big tree (strong marriage) that you spoke or sown on good ground (your faith in the Word). In the book of James 1:6–8, it says, "But let him ask in faith, with no doubting, for he who doubts is like a wave of the sea driven and tossed by the wind. For let not that man suppose that he will receive anything from the Lord: he is a double-minded man, unstable in all his ways."

Doubt cancels out faith, and faith cancels out doubt. Let faith in God's word rule in your life. The word of God was sent here for you to live an abundant life. The Lord Jesus was the Word made into flesh.

In the beginning was the Word, and the
Word was with God, and the Word was God. He

was in the beginning with God. All things were made through Him, and without Him nothing was made that was made. In Him was life, and the life was the light of men. He was in the world, and the world was made through Him, and the world did not know Him. He came to His own, and His own did not receive Him. But as many as received Him, to them He gave the right to become children of God, to those who believe in His name: And the Word became flesh (Jesus) and dwelt among us, and we beheld His glory, the glory as of the only begotten of the Father, full of grace and truth. (John 1:1–4, 10–12, 14)

His eyes were like a flame of fire, and on His head were many crowns. He had a name written that no one knew except Himself. He was clothed with a robe dipped in blood, and His name is called The Word of God. (Rev. 19:12–13)

Jesus is the Word of God. Everything that was created from the beginning was with words, which were created by the Lord Jesus the Word, and God said His Word shall not return to me void, but it shall accomplish what I please, and it shall prosper in the thing for which I sent it (Isa. 55:11). The Lord Jesus accomplished all that He was to accomplish and now He has left the church to carry out their part. All who have accepted Jesus, as their Lord and Savior will receive direction from the Holy Spirit on how to use their words. All of mankind has this ability to have what they say, but if you don't understand you have the God given ability to do so, don't understand who it was who created you, you will miss use the authority that was given to you. You may get what you want because your soul and body agree, but it may not be the will of God for you, because remember it only takes two witnesses to agree. But it takes three witnesses (spirit, soul and body) to be in the perfect will of God, and the perfect will of God is where you should want to be for God's abundant life for you.

The Principle of Giving

Your giving to others will be the seeds for financial increase.

> Whatever a man sows, that is what he will reap. (Gal. 6:7b)

> Give, and it will be given to you: good measure, pressed down, shaken together, and running over will be measured back to you. (Luke 6:38).

> Will a man rob God? Yet you have robbed me! But you say, "In what way have we robbed you?" In tithes and offerings. You are cursed with a curse, for you have robbed Me, Even this whole nation. Bring all the tithes into the storehouse, That there may be food in My house, And try Me now in this, Says the Lord of hosts, If I will not open for you the windows of heaven And pour out for you such blessing That there will not be room enough to receive it. (Mal. 3:8–10.)

"God so loved the world that He gave His only begotten Son." God had a heart first to help his people. What father would stand by and do nothing as their children were dying? Neither would the Father of all that are born again. He did something! The movie *The Passion of the Christ* by Mel Gibson shows a glimpse of what the Heavenly Father may have gone through when He gave His only begotten Son and when His Son, Jesus, laid down His life for the world. The principle God had created before time (seedtime and Harvest), He knew the seed sown would produce multiplied more. The Creator sowed His only begotten Son as a seed to inherit many more children.

If you don't give, you will not receive. That is why it is said that it is better to give than to receive. When you give you make others better and because of God's principle, you will also make yourself better. Seedtime and Harvest, whatever a man sows, that is what he will reap. If you need someone to love you, you show love toward someone else. If you need help in your business, you help someone in his or her business. If you need money, you give money to someone else. Whatever you sow on good ground, you will reap back multiplied more. Praise the Lord. As simple as that, sow no seed and get no harvest. The only way people are saved is by someone planting a seed of the Word God into them.

Faith comes by hearing and hearing by the
Word of God. (Rom. 10:17).

For God so love the world that He gave
His only begotten Son, that whoever believes
in Him should not perish but have eternal life.
(John 3:16)

We stated that God sowed His only begotten Son Jesus into the world to reap more children. God also sowed love into the world and is now reaping more love back in return. For if you love Him, the Bible says you will keep His commandments. John 14:15 says, "If you love Me, keep My commandments." All of you born again people that love God are a part of a seed He sown over two thousand years ago. Obeying His commandments is also to reap what you sow—two commandments, The Lord Jesus left will cover the original 10 commandments.

"Then one of them, a lawyer, asked Him
a question, testing Him, and saying. "Teacher,

which is the great commandment in the law?" Jesus said to him, "You shall love your God with all your heart, with all your soul, and with all your mind. "This is the first and great commandment. "And the second is like it: 'You shall love your neighbor as yourself.' "On these two commandments hang all the Law and the Prophets" (Matt. 22:35-40).

When you love the Lord your God, you are His seed indeed. When you love others, that seed of love now has been multiplied into the person that hears and receives the Gospel (Good News of Jesus Christ). The Lord blessed male and female, and God said to them, "Be Fruitful and multiply" (Gen. 1:28). The Creator intended that we increase after His kind, spirit, soul, and body. Adam and Eve broke that spiritual connection with the Creator, and Jesus came down to reconcile mankind back. Now, he has given us the ministry of reconciliation in order to multiply the people of God.

While the earth remains, Seedtime and harvest, Cold and heat, winter and summer, and day and night shall not cease. (Gen.8:22)

(Then Isaac sowed in that land, and reaped in the same year a hundredfold; and the Lord blessed him. The man began to prosper, and continued prospering until he became very prosperous; For he had possessions of flocks and possessions of herds and a great number of servants. So the Philistines envied him. (Gen. 26: 12)

Any believer reading this book right now may sow into the land (others) and reap, as did Isaac. In the book of Acts 10:34 (KJV) it says, "God is no respecter of persons." So if God did it for Isaac, the Lord our God will do it for you too. Look around and see those that are givers to others, they are receiving more back than they gave.

Oprah Winfrey is one of, if not, the richest lady in the world, but on the other hand, she is one of the biggest givers in the world. She reaps what she sows. I don't know if she is saved, but I do know the principle of seedtime and harvest, which is a principle for all the earth—saved or unsaved!

My formal Pastor, whom I highly respect dearly, is a giver. Some years ago, his church was raising money to build a church. The Lord put on his heart to give the money to other churches, some in need of help, and a well-off church. To make a long story short, the well-off church he gave to was building a new church. The founder of that church said, "The Holy Spirit told him to give my pastor the church they were moving from." Glory to God. The amazing thing about it is the well-off church still owed $900,000 on the old church.

The church members of that giving church raised money to pay towards the debt, and when it was all said and done, they had raised $810,000 toward paying off that debt before giving it to my formal pastor, Dr. Osborne Richards church. What the church gave to Dr. Richards church was worth 1.7 million dollars when they moved in, but all they paid was the $90,000 left over from what the giving church members had raised. Our God is good and all the time God is good. I believe had not my pastor had giving an offering to that church, not once, but on three occasions, we probably would not have received that church. It goes to show that the Lord God will open the windows of heaven and pour out a blessing on you that you will not have room enough to receive. Some nine years later, the church is worth 2.4 million dollars and debt free.

Someone reading this book may be saying, *What if I don't have anything to sow right now?* Well, sow what you do have, if no money, sow your time, serve in your church, and pray to the Lord that He will give you seed to sow. 2 Corinthians 9:10 says, "Now may He who supplies seed to the sower, and bread for food, supply and multiply the seed you have sown and increase the fruits of your righteousness." The people of Macedonia gave of themselves first.

Moreover, brethren, we make known to you
the grace of God bestowed on the churches of

> Macedonia: that in a great trial of affliction the abundance of their joy and their deep poverty abounded in the riches of their liberality. For I bear witness that according to their ability, yes and beyond their ability, they were freely willing, Imploring us with much urgency that we would receive the gift and the fellowship of the ministering to the saints. And not only as we had hoped, but they first gave themselves to the Lord, and then to us by the will of God. So we urged Titus, that as he had begun, so he would also complete this grace in you as well. But as you abound in everything—in faith, in speech, in knowledge, in all diligence, and in your love by diligence of others. For you know the grace of our Lord Jesus Christ, that though He was rich, yet for your sakes He became poor, that you through His poverty might become rich. (2 Cor. 8:1–9)

The people first gave what they had, which was their time and love. They ministered to the saints. Through their sowing of serving, they were blessed to sow with their financial support. I encourage you to read all of chapter 8 and 9 of 2 Corinthians. The Bible said, "Jesus became poor so that we may become rich." Think about it. The Lord Jesus came from heaven where "the streets are paved with gold, and the gates are made of pearls" (Rev. 21:21).

For the Lord Jesus to momentarily give up heaven to come to earth in the form of a baby then to walk as a man going about doing good—teaching, preaching, healing, casting out demons, and feeding the hungry—says a lot for His love for this world. For all His work of serving, the Lord Jesus has been exalted and is now at the right hand of power." Philippians 2:5–12 says:

> Let this mind be in you which was also in Christ Jesus, Who, being in the form of God did not consider it robbery to be equal with God?

But made Himself of no reputation, taking the form of a bondservant, and coming in the likeness of men. And being found in appearance as a man, He humbled Himself and became obedient to the point of death, even the death of the cross. Therefore God also has highly exalted Him and given Him the name which is above every name. That at the name of Jesus every knee should bow, of those in heaven, and of those on earth, and of those under the earth. And that every tongue should confess that Jesus Christ is Lord, to the glory of God the Father. Therefore, my beloved, as you have always obeyed, not as in my presence only, but now much more in my absence, work out your own salvation with fear and trembling.

Our Lord and Savior has shown us, in His Holy Word, how He became poor for us and served so that we would become rich. He too became rich again, but even more so because God the Father has given Him all power, on earth and in heaven.

The eyes of your understanding being enlightened; that you may know what is the hope of His calling, what are the riches of the glory of his inheritance in the saints, And what is the exceeding greatness of His power toward us who believe, according to the working of His mighty power. Which He worked in Christ when He raised Him from the dead and seated Him at His right hand in the heavenly places. Far above all principality and power and might and dominion, and every name that is named, not only in this age but also in that which is to come. And He put all things under His feet, and gave Him to be head over all things to the church. Which is

His body, the fullness of Him who fills all in all.
(Eph. 1:18–21)

And as He is rich, so is His body, for we are seated with Him. We, the church (children of God), are above all principalities, power, might, and dominion here on the earth with our Lord and Savior. Jesus the Christ!

Hallelujah. Thank you, Lord Jesus.

Recognizing the Power of Words and Agreements

Let us look at a true example from the Word of God, dealing with the power of your words and the power of agreement.

> Now the whole earth had one language and one speech. And it came to pass, as they journeyed from the east, that they found a plain in the land of Shinar, and they dwelt there. Then they <u>said</u> to one another, "Come, let us make bricks and bake them thoroughly." They had brick for stone, and they had asphalt for mortar. And they <u>said</u>, "Come, let us build ourselves a city, and a tower whose top is in the heavens; let us make a name for ourselves, lest we be scattered abroad over the face of the whole earth." But the Lord came down to see the city and the tower which the sons of men had built. And the Lord said, "Indeed the people are one and they all have one language, and this is what they begin to do; **now nothing** that they propose to do will be withheld from them. "Come, let Us go down and there confuse their <u>language</u>, that they may not understand one another's <u>speech</u>." So the Lord scattered them abroad from there over the face of all the earth, and they ceased building the city.

Therefore its name is called Babel, because there
the Lord confused the <u>language</u> of all the earth;
and from there the Lord scattered them abroad
over the face of all the earth. (Gen. 11:1–9)

Did you see it? What the people set their heart to do
(believed) and their speech (words) allowed them to do whatever
they said. These people were not even saved back then. In verse 6,
it was said now nothing that they propose to do will be withheld
from them. Why? It is because of their words and the power of
agreement with one another. Words enable us to communicate
with one another. How may we help those in need if we cannot understand them? God scattered them because their hearts
were not on Him, but on themselves wanting to make a name for
themselves. God gave us His Word to accomplish His plans and
purposes, which is to increase and multiply after His own kind.
Everything God made was good, and it benefited the plan of God.
Even when God said multiply.

He spoke this Word before Adam and Eve sinned. He didn't
intend for them to multiply after their sinful nature. That is why
Jesus (Word) was sent to put us back on God's plan to multiply after
His own kind. John 1:12 says, "But as many as received Him, to
them He gave the right to become children of God, to those who
believe in His name." The only way to use your words properly, in
the way it was designed to be used, is to use the Words in the Bible
(God's manual for mankind) in the name of Jesus. The Lord scattered the people who used their words foolishly but blessed those
that use them wisely.

Whatever you say will affect your environment. Anyone can
operate an automobile if they have basic training on one, but the
person who reads the owner's manual will be able to take full advan-
tage of all the equipment on the automobile. The same holds true
to people being of the creation of the Most High God. He created
you, so therefore, all those that read His Bible (manual), and apply
themselves to it, will be the ones who will benefit on all that God
has for them in God's own way. The people of Babel did not have a

written word to go by as we do in today's time. So we have no excuse for operating our words in the wrong manner or with wrong motives. We have to realize that all things are possible to those that believe in God. Those people who believe on God for increase will have no limits on what God will do for them.

Genesis 18:14a says, "Is anything too hard for the Lord?" Mark 9:23 says, "Jesus said to him, 'If you can believe, all things are possible to him who believes.'"

To back up these words from the Lord, He says in Matthew 24:35, "Heaven and earth will past away, but My words will by no means pass away."

> So shall my word be that goes forth from My mouth; It shall not return to Me Void, But it shall accomplish what I please, And it shall prosper in the thing for which I sent it. (Isa. 55:11)

> In hope of eternal life which God, who cannot lie, promised before time began. (Titus 1:2)

There you have it, the infallible truth. The word of God is full proof. There are no other things that are as sure and proven as the Word of God. Remember back in John 1? Jesus is the Word, and the Word is what created the heavens and the earth. When you are born again, the Word comes on the inside of you, but you still must abide in the Word. John 15:7 says, "If you abide in Me, and My words abide in you, you will ask what you desire, and it shall be done for you." Glory Hallelujah (praise the Lord), did you see that? If we abide in Him, and His Words abide in us, we may have what we ask of Him and it shall be done. Praise God.

The Lord our God wants you to have the things you desire. It's mentioned in the Bible so many times. If it were not so, the Lord would not have told us so. Our God wants you to be healed, debt free, in good health, prosperous, in your right minds, and just plain living the abundant life. What father would want to see their children broke, sick, depressed, and barely getting by? The answer is no father would want this for his own children.

> Ask, and it will be given to you; seek, and you will find; knock, and it will be opened to you. "For everyone who asks receives, and he who seeks finds, and to him who knocks it will be opened. "Or what man is there among you who, if his son asks for bread, will give him a stone? "Or if he asks for a fish, will he give him a serpent? "If you then, being evil, know how to give good gifts to your children, how much more will your Father who is in heaven give good things to those who ask Him! (Matt. 7:7–12)

Say this out loud, "My God in heaven gives good things to those who ask of Him." Say this out loud, "My God in heaven gives good things to those who ask of Him." Say this out loud, "My God in heaven gives good things to those who ask of Him."

Now, child of God, ask Him for what you want, and when you ask, believe that you have already received it. Remember, first thing first, if you have anything against anyone, forgive him or her, and your Father, who is in heaven, will forgive you. Right now, this moment, you believe and ask the Father for what you desire of Him.

Repeat it seven times, and allow the words to penetrate your spirit, sowing on a strong foundation, then watering your words with faith. Every time you see or hear doubt (weeds), cancel it out with water (faith). Pick up the Word of God, and read what it says about your situation.

> So then faith comes by hearing, and hearing by the word of God. (Rom. 10:17)

> But what does it say? "The word is near you, in your mouth and in your heart." (Rom. 10:8)

That is the word of faith in which we preach.

Child of God if you stand on the word of God in faith, and it tells you that you may call those things that be not as though they were, you will have whatever you say. Then you keep calling it what you want it to be, and not what it appears to be. Adam named every animal and insect "whatever he called it was its name," you and I have the same ability to call it what we want it to be. Amen!

Keep in mind—the big tree doesn't always come right up. The best trees will take a longer time to grow, which will require more water (faith) and building a stronger foundation. Never give up and never give in.

> My brethren, count it all joy when you fall into various trails. Knowing that the testing of your faith produces patience. But let patience have its perfect work, that you may be perfect and <u>complete</u>, lacking NOTHING.

> If any of you lacks wisdom, let him ask of God, who gives to all liberally and without reproach, and it will be given to him. But let him ask in faith, with no doubting, for he who doubts is like a wave of the sea driven and tossed by the wind. for let not that man suppose that he will receive anything from the Lord; He is a double-minded man, unstable in all his ways. (James 1:2–8)

Again, we say never give up and never give in.

You must stand on your prayers to God the Father in the name of the Lord Jesus the Christ.

The devil will come and try to steal your seed (word) that was sown. But don't you let him, you are a child of God, and you have all of God's power working in you, through you, and for you. Also remember, you will "do all things through Christ Jesus that strengthens you" (Phil. 4:13).

The Most Powerful Words that One May Say

In the beginning, when God created man, the first thing God did was to speak over his life. The first thing God assigned man to do was to speak over the animals (Adam named the animals in Genesis 2:19). The first thing one must do to be born again (give their life to Christ Jesus) is to use their mouth. John 3:3 says, "Jesus answered and said to him, 'Most assuredly, I say to you, unless one is born again, he cannot see the kingdom of God.'" The reason that we must be born again is because of the sin nature that we inherited from Adam and Eve when their words caused them to sin (agreed with the words of the serpent). Now in the New Testament, the ultimate example of the power of our words is found in the most important thing to mankind and that is their salvation (being born again).

In order to be a child of God and not His creation only is to give your life to Him. The way to eternal (everlasting life) salvation (saved) is through King Jesus. The way to be born again is found in Holy Bible. Romans 10:9–10 says, "That if you <u>confess</u> (words) with your mouth the Lord Jesus and believe in your heart that God has raised Him from the dead, you will be saved. For with the heart one believes unto righteousness, and with the mouth <u>confession</u> (words) is made unto salvation."

Did you see it? You must use your words in order to receive the greatest gift God has for you, which is to be born again. Making you not only God's creation, but also His only begotten children. You cannot convince me otherwise that the power is not in our words.

You are saved by your belief on Him and the words you speak that you believe in Him (Holy God).

There are just so many testimonies, so many examples of science and historical proofs that tell you that every Word of God is true. There have been countless recordings of miraculous healings taken place because of people having faith and speaking the words of God. Success story after success story of how people have said they read the Word, and the Word they spoke and believed on came to pass. You cannot get around it. The power is in your words!

The Power comes from the Holy Spirit

The power that comes from receiving the Holy Spirit is given through your tongue (words).

Jesus told His disciple to wait for the power from the Father when the Holy Spirit comes on them.

> And He said to them, it is not for you to know times or seasons which the Father has put in His own authority. But you shall receive power when the Holy Spirit has come upon you; and you shall be witnesses to Me in Jerusalem, and in all Judea and Samaria, and to the end of the earth." These all continued with one accord in prayer and supplication, with the women and Mary the mother of Jesus, and with His brothers. And in those days Peter stood up in the midst of the disciples (altogether the number of names was about a hundred and twenty). (Acts 1:7–8, 14–15)

> When the Day of Pentecost had fully come, they were all with one accord in one place. And suddenly there came a sound from heaven as of a rushing mighty wind, and it filled the whole house where they were sitting. Then there

appeared to them divided <u>tongues</u>, as of fire, and one sat upon each of them. And they were all filled with the Holy Spirit and began to speak (words) with other <u>tongues</u> (words), as the Spirit gave them utterance. (Acts 2:1–4)

The experience that these 120 people had was the evidence for them receiving a spiritual gift (power) from on high. Since one may not see this kind of power with the eye, how would they know if they received it? Since Jesus understood that these people were aware of the old scripture and knew that whenever the Spirit of God would come on them in the old scriptures, they would begin to prophesize (speak words).

Then the Spirit of the Lord will come upon you, and you will prophesy (speak words) with them and be turned into another man. (1 Sam. 10:6)

Then the Lord came down in the cloud, and spoke to him, and took of the Spirit that was upon him, and placed the same upon the seventy elders; and it happened, when the Spirit rested upon them, that they prophesied, although they never did so again. (Num. 11:25)

And it shall come to pass afterward That I will pour out My Spirit on all flesh; Your sons and your daughters shall prophesy, Your old men shall dream dreams, your young men shall see visions. (Joel 2:28)

It was evident that the people in Jesus's day could identify with the power being transferred through the tongue because they had been taught about it all their lives. So on the day of Pentecost, they have seen what appeared to be tongues and one rested on each one of them. They began to speak in an unknown tongue. This was the New Testament evidence that they had received the power that Jesus spoke of. Because it had been made known these "believers were speaking in a language that they had never learned" (Acts 2:5–8). After Pentecost, people that were there knew they had the power of God inside of them. They went boldly proclaiming all over the region that Jesus was the Christ.

Remember Peter? The one in the Bible who had denied Christ three times before the rooster crowed. Luke 22:34 says, "Then He said, 'I tell you, Peter, the rooster shall not crow this day before you will deny three times that you know Me.'" Let us pick up now in Luke 22:55:

> Now when they had kindled a fire in the midst of the courtyard and sat down together, Peter sat among them. And a certain servant girl, seeing him as he sat by the fire, looked intently at him and said, "This man was also with Him (speaking of Jesus)." But he denied Him, saying, "Woman, I do not know Him." And after a little while another saw him and said, "You also are of them." But Peter said, "Man, I am not!" Then after about an hour had passed, another confidently affirmed, saying, "Surely this fellow also was with Him, for he is a Galilean." But Peter said, "Man, I do not know what you are saying!" Immediately, while he was still speaking, the rooster crowed. And the Lord turned and looked at Peter. Then Peter remembered the <u>word</u> of the Lord, how He had said to him, "Before the rooster crows, you will deny Me three times.

We see again how your words and the words of others may affect you. The main thing I want for you to see is that Peter was afraid and had no power at this time.

We will pick back up in the Word of God with Jesus knowing the results of our words and then leads Peter into canceling out his words, denying Him those three times.

> So when they had eaten breakfast, Jesus said to Simon Peter, "Simon, son of Jonah, do you love Me more than these?" He said to Him, "Yes, Lord; you know that I love you." He said to him, "Feed My lambs." He said to him again a second time, "Simon, son of Jonah, do you love Me?" He said to Him, "Yes, Lord; you know that I love you." He said to him, "Tend My sheep." He said to him the third time, "Simon, son of Jonah, do you love Me?" Peter was grieved because He said to him the third time, "Do you love Me?" And he said to Him, "Lord, You know all things; you know that I love you." Jesus said to him, "Feed My sheep." (John 21:15–17)

Yes, the Lord Jesus did know Peter loved Him, but the words of denying Him Peter spoke had to be cancelled out with words. The Lord Jesus couldn't even do it without Peter canceling it out himself. For Jesus said, "If we deny Him, He would deny us before the Father."

> But whoever denies Me before men, him I will also deny before My Father who is in heaven. (Matt. 10:33)

So Peter was afraid after Jesus had been taken into custody that the soldiers would take him also. After Jesus had died and rose again, the Lord Jesus told them to wait for the power, and that is what they did. They waited in the upper room. As we read in Acts 2, they were all filled with the Holy Spirit and began to speak in unknown tongues. Now, let us look at what happened after they understood they had the power.

> Now Peter and John went up together to the temple at the hour of prayer, the ninth hour. And a certain man lame from his mother's womb was carried, whom they laid daily at the gate of the temple which is called Beautiful, to ask alms from those who entered the temple. Who, seeing Peter and John about to go into the temple, asked for alms. And fixing his eyes on him, with John, Peter said, "Look at us." So he gave them his attention, expecting to receive something from them. Then Peter said, "Silver and gold I do not have, but what I do have I give you: In the name of Jesus Christ of Nazareth, rise up and walk." And he took him by the right hand and lifted him up, and immediately his feet and ankle bones received Strength. So he, leaping up, stood and walked and entered the temple with them-walking, leaping, and praising God. (Acts 3:1–8)

Here we see that now Peter and John are going up to the temple with boldness, and even though they don't have any money, they realize they have something more valuable than money. They had the power (Holy Spirit) and the Word of the Lord. In verse four, Peter said to the man, "Rise up and walk in the Name of Jesus." These are powerful words. Even though at the time they had no money, but they knew they had King Jesus and the Holy Spirit in them.

By now, you know that He is the Word, and if the Word abides in you, you shall ask what you will, and it shall be done unto you. Let us look further in how being filled with the Holy Spirit with the evidence of speaking in tongues was evident.

> Now as they spoke to the people, the priests, the captain of the temple, and the Sadducees came upon them. Being greatly disturbed that they taught the people and preached in Jesus the resurrection from the dead. And they laid hands

on them, and put them in custody until the next day, for it was already evening. However, many of those who heard the word believed; and the number of the men came to be about five thousand. And it came to pass, on the next day, that their rulers, elders, and scribes. As well as Anna's the high priest, Caiaphas, John, and Alexander, and as many as were of the family of the high priest, were gathered together at Jerusalem. And when they had set them in the midst, they asked, by what power of by what name have you done this?" Then Peter, filled with the Holy Spirit, said to them, Rulers of the people and elders of Israel: "If we this day are judged for a good deed done to a helpless man, by what means he has been made well, "let it be known to you all, and to all the people of Israel, that by the name of Jesus Christ of Nazareth, whom you crucified, whom God raised from the dead, by Him this man stands here before you whole. "This is the 'stone which was rejected by you builders, which has become the chief cornerstone.' "Nor is there salvation in any other, for there is no other name under heaven given among men by which we must be saved." Now when they saw the boldness of Peter and John, and perceive that they were uneducated and untrained men, they marveled. And they realized that they had been with Jesus. And seeing the man who had been healed standing with them, they could say nothing against it. But when they had commanded them to go aside out of the council, they conferred among themselves. Saying, "What shall we do to these men? For, indeed, that a notable miracle has been done through them is evident to all who dwell in Jerusalem, and we cannot deny it. "But so that it spreads no further among the people, let us severely threaten them that from now on they <u>speak</u> to no man in this name." So they called them and commanded them not to <u>speak</u> at all nor teach in the name of Jesus. But Peter and John answered and <u>said </u>to them, "Whether it is right in the sight of God to listen to you more than to God, you judge. <u>"For we cannot but speak the things which we have seen and heard</u>." So when they had further threatened them, they let them go, finding no way of punishing them, because of the people, since they all glorified God for what had been done. (Acts 4:1–21)

You now see the boldness of Peter, keep in mind, Peter had denied the Lord Jesus and said he wasn't one of his disciples when they had taken the Lord to be crucified. Scripture says, "And Simon Peter stood and warmed himself. They said therefore unto him, art not thou also one of His disciples? He denied it, and said, I am not. One of the servants of the high priest, being his kinsman whose ear Peter cut off, saith, did not I see thee in the garden with him? Peter then denied again: and immediately the cock crew" (John 18:25–27).

But after the Holy Spirit had come upon them with the evidence of speaking in an unknown tongue, Peter knew he had the power of God in him, and he spoke boldly throughout the region on the teachings of the Lord Jesus. For even after being beaten and warned not to again speak on Jesus Name, Peter told them that "they would rather do and (speak) what was right in the sight of God then to listen to them." What we see here is not only do your words have power, but also when you are saved and filled with the Holy Spirit, you have the boldness to speak when being led by the Holy Spirit anywhere. "You would receive power when the Holy Spirit comes upon you and you shall be witnesses for Jesus all over the earth" (Acts 1:8). People don't just have power (authority) with your words, but use your words in the power that they were created for. Genesis

1:28 says, "Then God blessed them, 'Be fruitful and multiply; fill the earth and subdue it; have dominion.'"

You and I have been blessed. We have been destined to increase. So many times, in His Word (Bible), the Lord is showing us how to use what He has given us, seed! Yes, seed. Our words are seed, whatever we say, believe that we have received it, and we shall have it. The Lord wanted to show the believers that they received this power that he instructed them to wait on. He packaged the power up in what they could identify with, tongues. Did you see it back when we were reading in Acts 2:3? "Then there appeared (came into sight) to them divided tongues, as of fire, and one sat upon each of them."

This verse verifies that they received the power, and the speaking in tongues was the evidence of them receiving the promise. How else would they have known they had received the spiritual promise unless it came with evidence? The speaking in tongues are that evidence you are filled with the Holy Ghost.

What is described here is a visual scene. They saw whether in the spiritual or the natural realm tongues as having fire on them, and one of the tongues sat upon each individual there. Fire also represented power in the New Testament because John the Baptist said that one would come, speaking of the Lord Jesus. Let us read it for ourselves.

> I indeed baptize you with water unto repentance, but He who is coming after me is mightier than I, whose sandals I am not worthy to carry. He will baptize you with the Holy Spirit and fire. (Matt.3:11)

Jesus also spoke these words:

> And being assembled together with them, He (Jesus) commanded them not to depart from Jerusalem, but to wait for the Promise of the Father, "which," He said, "you have heard from Me; "For John truly baptized with water, but you

shall be baptized with the Holy Spirit not many days from now." (Acts 1:4–5)

Behold, I send the Promise of My Father upon you; but tarry (wait) in the city of Jerusalem until you are endued (provided) with power from on high. (Luke 24:49)

The people were waiting for the power from on high, and it was to be accompanied by the Holy Spirit. So when they saw the tongues and fire, they knew this had to be it, so they began to speak. When they spoke, it was with other tongues. The Lord had to show them that this was the power that the old prophets had when the Holy Spirit was with *them*, but the new thing that the Father had for them was the Holy Spirit *in them*. John 7:37–39 says, "On the last day, that great day of the feast, Jesus stood and cried out, saying, 'If anyone thirsts, let him come to Me and drink. He who believes in me, as the Scripture has said, out of his heart will Flow Rivers of living water.' But this He spoke concerning the Spirit, whom those believing in Him would receive; for the Holy Spirit was not yet given, because Jesus was not yet glorified." This the Lord Jesus was speaking of after His death and resurrection would come to the believers.

The power is in your mouth to increase, and if you don't have the confidence to use it on your own, the Lord will send you a helper to help you use your God given authority as He purposed for you. *John 15:26–27 says,* "But when the Helper comes, whom I shall send to you from the Father, the Spirit of truth (Holy Spirit) who proceeds from the Father, He will testify of Me. "And you also will bear witness, because you have been with Me from the beginning." John 16:23 says, "And in that day you will ask Me nothing. Most assuredly, I say to you, whatever you ask the Father in My name He will give you."

Now the people had assurance that they would have the authority in them to ask for whatever they wanted, and it would be done unto them. You, who are reading this book, were destined to read this book in order for you to realize what you have been seeking for (a better joy-able life) is available to you now. You are entitled to ask for it and receive it by His Words and you speaking and believing His Words. You will make it; yes, you will make it, and you were destined to increase in the name of Lord Jesus.

God your Father is showing you every way possibly for you to see and then do what He has commanded you to do. When we look bad, our Father looks bad. Just think about it, if you are telling people that the Creator of the world is your Father, they are expecting for you to be living well, conducting yourself well, handling adverse situations well, and increasing in all that you do. When you are not operating in a blessed favored life, it reflects back on who we say we are. It's not God's fault but the fault of His Children for not using His Word.

He's given you everything you need to succeed. He's given you the Lord Jesus, He's given you the Holy Spirit, He's given you examples, and most importantly, He's given you His instructions (Holy Bible). You cannot fail! You will not fail. You were destined to increase. I don't care what has happened before now or what is going on now, you have the ability right now to change your environment. Just speak what you want, and believe it when you speak it. If weeds of doubt creep up, get into the Word of God, and water it again, and again with faith. You are created in the image of God. You are a child of the Most High God. "For greater is He that is in you than he that is in the world, you can do all things through Christ Jesus that strengthens you."

You are of God, little children, and have overcome them, because He who is in you is greater than he who is in the world. (1 John 4:4)

I can do all things through Christ, which strengthens me. (Phil. 4:13)

There Is Power in the Word of God

The full proof way for you to know that what you say will come to pass for those that may have trouble understanding that your words do create. You stick to speaking the Words in the Holy Bible. The Lord said, "His Word would not return to Him void. So if you speak His word and again water it with faith. It will prosper into the thing that it was called to prosper in."

> For as the rain comes down, and the snow from heaven, and do not return there, But water the earth, And make it bring forth and bud, that it may give seed to the sower And bread to the eater. So shall My word be that goes forth from My mouth; It shall not return to Me void, But it shall accomplish what I please, And it shall prosper in the thing for which I sent it. (Isa. 55:10, 11)

> This Book of the Law shall not depart from your mouth, but you shall meditate in it day and night, that you may observe to do according to all that is written in it. For then you will make your way prosperous, and then you will have good success. Have I not commanded you? Be strong and of good courage; do not be afraid, nor

be dismayed, for the Lord your God is with you
wherever you go. (Josh. 1:8–9)

Meditating on the Word of God produces faith (waters).
Speaking the Word of God produces good success. It was commanded to do what was written in the Word (Holy Bible) and, for
us to do it not being afraid, but of courage, knowing that the Lord
our God is with you wherever you shall go. Isn't that powerful? You
have been assured that the word will work if we work it. So there are
no excuses, not your skin color, not where you were raised, not your
age, or education. We all have been created in the image and likeness
of God our Creator. The Most High God stated that everything He
made was good. Don't tell yourself anything else, and don't let anyone else make you think anything else. The Bible says, "If God is for
us, who can be against us?" (Rom. 8:31b)

No devil in hell or anyone else can succeed against you. No
valley, no mountains, no storms of life, no lion dens, no burning fur-
naces—nothing can come between you and what God has called you
to be (blessed and highly favored), nothing, nobody, only ourselves.
We have the ability to fulfill our destiny. God said it, God did it, and
it is done!

You have the power in your mouth, and if you are born again,
the power (Holy Spirit) is in you and directing you. Give the Lord
a shout of praise right now, for He is worthy of the praise! He has
given you all what you will ever need to fulfill His plans and purpose.
Which includes saving souls, being blessed, and increasing in everything you do until He comes to get us. Hallelujah! Glory to God. It
is in His word that states He will give you your desires.

Delight yourself also in the Lord, and He
shall give you the desires of your heart. (Ps. 37:4)

Now this is the confidence that we have in
Him, that if we ask anything according to His will
(bible is His will), He Hears us. And if we know
that He hears us, whatever we ask, we know that

we have the petitions that we have asked of Him.
(1 John 5:14–15)

> And whatever you ask in My name, that I
> will do, that the Father may be glorified in the
> Son. If you ask anything in My name, I will do
> it. (John 14:13–14)

When you desire from the Father, speak the Word of God (Holy Bible), and do so in the name of the Lord Jesus. The Lord Jesus said that you shall have whatsoever you ask for. The Lord our God has given us so many tools to use in order to increase in this life. People, we cannot lose with God on our side. If Daniel could be thrown in a lion's den (1 Sam. 6) and not be harmed, how about you? If the three Hebrew boys could be thrown into a fiery furnace (Dan. 3) and not be consumed by it, how about you believing your way out of your trials and difficulties. If David could kill the giant in his life (1 Sam. 17), why can't you kill the giants in your own life? God is able to do it in your life when you are born again (believe and confess the Lord Jesus as your savior and water baptism). You now have the Power of God in you to do all He destined you to do. Glory to God!

There are many more we could name, but the just of it all is because they trusted in God and spoke of their deliverer (God), they were saved. Now how about you? I don't know if you are going through something right now, but if you are, trust in your Heavenly Father. Ask for what you want, and do it all in the name of the Lord Jesus. You need help in your finances, ask in the name of the Lord Jesus, and please wait until your breakthrough comes. You need your body healed, ask and wait (expecting) in faith; it is done in the Lord Jesus. Whatever it may be, marriage problems or depression, our God is more than able. Scripture says, "Now to Him (God) who is able to do exceeding abundantly above all that we ask or think, according to the power that works in us" (Eph. 3:20).

Creating Your own Environment

You have the ability to create your own environment (surroundings) or change it. There are three main sources that contribute to what kind of environment you will choose.

1. Your words—the things that you allow or choose to say.
2. What you think or what you choose to think.
3. What you do or what you choose to do.

We will explore the three in detail through the word of our Lord God.

Creating Your Environment Through Your Words

Up to this point, we have been spending most of our time talking about what you say will determine what you get. So just to add to what has already been said. Let us look at what James said about your words (tongue).

> For we all stumble in many things, if anyone does not stumble in word, he is a perfect man, able also to bridle the whole body. Indeed, we put bits in horse's mouths that they may obey us, and we turn their whole body. Look also at ships: although they are so large and are driven by fierce winds, they are turned by a very small rudder wherever the pilot desires. Even so the

tongue is a little member and boasts great things. See how great a forest a little fire kindles! And the tongue is a fire, a world of iniquity. The tongue is so set among our members that it defiles the whole body, and sets on fire the course of nature; and it is set on fire by hell. For every kind of beast and bird, of reptile and creature of the sea, is tamed and has been tamed by mankind.

But no man can tame the tongue. It is an unruly evil, full of deadly poison. With it we bless our God and Father, and with it we curse men, who have been made in the similitude of God. Out of the same mouth proceed blessing and cursing. My brethren, these things ought not to be so. Does a spring send forth fresh water and bitter from the same opening? Can a fig tree, my brethren, bear olives, or a grapevine bear figs? Thus no spring yields both salt water and fresh. "Who is wise and understanding among you? Let him show by good conduct that his works are done in the meekness of wisdom. (James 3:2–13)

James stated that within your mouth, you have the ability to control your whole body. You may speak to yourself and tell yourself what to do. You also may choose what you say to others, which is having control over your tongue. People respond to things we say—positive or negative. Remember back in the earlier part of this book, your words are like seed; whatever you say will produce a harvest. If good words are spoken that bless others, then you in turn will receive good things or blessings back. If bad words are spoken that curses, then you, in turn, will receive bad things or curses back. Whatever a man sows that is what he will receive.

In the story of Abraham, when tested by God, Abraham spoke words of what he wanted to happen, verses what God had told him. Abraham did not know it was a test, but he did know the God he served and that if God did take his son, God was able to bring him back again. Let us pick up where Abraham uses his words to create his environment, which was the environment that the Lord our God has destined for him to create.

Now it came to pass after these things that God tested Abraham, and said to him, "Abraham!" And he said, "Here I am." Then He said, "Take now your son, your only son Isaac, whom you love, and go to the land of Moriah, and offer him there as a burnt offering on one of the mountains of which I shall tell you." So Abraham rose early in the morning and saddled his donkey, and took two of his young men with him, and Isaac his son; and he split the wood for the burnt offering, and arose and went to the place of which God had told him. Then on the third day Abraham lifted his eyes and saw the place afar off. And Abraham said to his young men, "Stay here with the donkey; the lad and I will go yonder and worship, and we will come back to you." So Abraham took the wood of the burnt offering and laid it on Isaac his son; and he took the fire in his hand, and a knife, and the two of them went together. But Isaac spoke to Abraham his father and said, "My father!" And he said, "Here I am, my son." Then he said, "Look, the fire and the wood, but where is the lamb for a burnt offering?" And Abraham said, "My son, God will provide for Himself the lamb for a burnt offering." So the two of them went together. Then they came to the place of which God had told him. And Abraham built an altar there and placed the wood in order; and he bound Isaac his son and laid him on the altar, upon the wood. And Abraham stretched out his hand and took the knife to slay his son. But the Angel of the LORD called to him from heaven and said, "Abraham, Abraham!" So he said, "Here I am." And He said, "Do not lay your hand on the lad, or do anything to him; for now I know that you fear God, since you have not withheld your son, your only son, from Me. Then Abraham lifted his eyes and looked, and there behind him was a ram caught in a thicket by its horns. So Abraham went and took the ram and offered it up for a burnt offering instead of his son. (Gen. 22: 1–13).

The very words that Abraham spoke in verse 5, when he told the men that we (he and the lad) would come back to you, are exactly what happened. As we read on, the Lord provided an offering in place of Isaac (the son). It shouldn't matter to you what the test or what the trial looks like. You need to speak what you want, rather than what you see, feel, or hear. The power is in your words to create the environment that God destined for you from the very beginning. In Hebrews 4:12, "it talks about the word "being living, powerful, and sharper than any two-edged sword piercing even to the division of soul and spirit, and of joints and marrow, and is a discerner of the thoughts and intents of the heart." The word of God is powerful, and because you were created in his image and likeness, your words are powerful too.

Creating Your Environment with Your Thinking

There have been books written on the power of thinking. The Bible says in Proverbs 23:7a, "For as he thinks in his heart so is he." The very thoughts that you have will affect what you say and what you will do. That is why your thinking is considered to be one of the causes to creating your environment.

If you think you are sick, in many cases, you will become sick unless you cancelled out those thoughts with other thoughts or with other words of healing. Our thinking affects how you feel about yourself and how you feel about others.

When you know who you are and who your maker is, you should see yourself in the way He sees you. The Creator said that you are "fearfully and wonderfully made" (Ps. 139:14). Everything that He made He said was "very good" (Gen. 1:31). Before you were conceived, He knew you. Jeremiah 1:5 says, "Before I formed you in the womb I knew you; before you were born I sanctified you; I ordained you a prophet to the nations."

> I will praise you, for I am fearfully and wonderfully made, Marvelous are your works, and that my soul knows very well. (Ps. 139:14)

> Then God saw everything that He had made, and indeed it was very good. So the evening and the morning were the sixth day. (Gen. 1:31)

Who would dare tell God that what He made was bad when God said everything He made was very good? So you are very good, that is the way you were created. All you need now is to bring it out of yourself, and the way to do that is by using the principles in the Bible that God gave you. If you obey, you will have the good things of the land, you will sow and reap as the Lord our God intended you to. He sent His only begotten Son, the Lord Jesus, into the world to die for the world because you meant that much to Him. God sowed love into the world and received you back. So when we sow love, we receive back love. I'm just in the belief that before God spoke us into existence, he thought about how good we would be, how He would love us, and how we would love Him. So God whom created seedtime and harvest, and I believe He said I will make a sacrifice and sow my only begotten Son (Jesus), and receive back a great harvest (saved souls) for my seed (only begotten Son). John 14:15 says, "If you love me keep My commandments."

To keep the Lord's commandments is to show Him that you love Him. When love is defined it usually referred to as having a strong affection for another, but agape (Greek word) love, on the other hand, is doing something for others. God says if you love Him, do something, be obedient, and keep His commandments. If you love someone, you won't do anything to hurt them. God so loved the world that He gave His only begotten Son, even though the world was full of sinners. Another reason to love God is when keeping His commandments, you will be fulfilling your purpose on the earth. God created you to increase what He had started and bring worship and service for the work of the kingdom. Since we were created for this very reason, this is the only way for mankind to feel completed and to know they have a purpose (a destiny) to love God and to love others as God loves us.

So by thinking of yourself as having a purpose (increasing the kingdom of our Lord by multiplying), in whatever gift or talent God has given you knowing why you are here, brings clarity to who you are (a child of the Most High God). As we have heard so many times, the devil's job is to steal your purpose and plans that the Lord our God has for you. That is why it is vital that we obey the commands of the Lord, for it is the only way to defeat the enemy and to live out our lives in peace and Joy. In the book of Nehemiah, it says, "The Joy of the Lord is your strength." Understand this verse, being a child of God gives you joy that you may call on the Lord Jesus at any time and with any need, knowing this gives strength to us in the Lord Jesus. We are weak, but He is Strong, and we may have joy about our loving strong Savoir. We may speak a change to come in our circumstances because of His sacrifice and because of His Word. Praise the Lord.

As mentioned earlier, when you do the will of God, your spirit is hearing from God. The spirit, soul, and body are at one with one another, so not only are you getting what you say, but it will also be in line with the plan of God for your life.

> For the kingdom of God is not meat and drink; but righteousness (right standing with God), and peace, and joy in the Holy Ghost. (Rom. 14:1

The thief does not come except to steal,
and to kill, and to destroy, I (Jesus) have come
that they may have life, and that they may have it
more abundantly. (John10:10)

We should follow after the Lord Jesus, for He has come to give us life, while the thief (devil) has come to take away from us disguised as something good, while being something bad.

When my oldest daughter was five years old, she came in from school one day, and I asked her how her day at school went. She replied, "I had a great day." I asked her what happened.

She replied, "I didn't lose any apples, and I didn't get my name on the chalkboard."

To explain what she meant, the teacher used a discipline method by giving the children stickers that resembled an apple.

If the children act in a way that does not line up with classroom rules, they will lose an apple. The previous week, my daughter had lost an apple one day and got her name written on the chalkboard two other days, which is another method for discipline. Yes, she had a tough week that week. So I asked her what the difference between how last week went and this week. She replied, "I didn't get in trouble, and the teacher gave me a candy cane for being good."

I ask her then what made her not get in trouble this time. She said, "When I was in trouble at home, sitting in my room, I thought that if I played at playtime at school and worked at work time, I would not get into any trouble."

I said, "That sounds like a great plan you had."

Then I asked her which week she enjoyed the best. She said the one in which she did not lose any apples or have her name written on the board. She went on to say that she wanted to go through the whole year without getting into trouble. She enjoyed how her day went, enjoyed her teacher's response, and enjoyed the response of her parents. My daughter's thinking mixed with her words and actions caused her environment to change. What about yours? The Lord Jesus said we should have childlike faith.

It all came about for my daughter keeping her apples by her thinking that she wanted to do better and what she would need to do in order to do better. She thought about it and then she went to school and acted on it. What an example for all of God's children. In order to have a great day, we must think we will have a great day then act like we are having a great day. I used to hear some say "fake it until you make it." Well, I hear the voice of the Lord, saying, "Sow it until you receive it." When we think well about ourselves, when we speak well about ourselves, and when we do those good things for others and ourselves, we reap what we sow. We create our environment with these three things: *speak, think, and what we do.*

> I beseech you therefore, brethren, by the mercies of God, that you present your bodies a living sacrifice, holy, acceptable to God, which is your reasonable service. And do not be conformed to this world, but be transformed by the renewing of your <u>mind (thinking)</u>, that you may prove what is that good and acceptable and perfect will of God. (Rom. 12:1–2)

The world has its way of thinking, which is to satisfy the flesh as with Adam and Eve. Our God has called us to reign with Him on the earth and in the heavens. We are in the world, but now that we are saved, we are not of this world. Our thinking now should line up with God's kingdom thinking. We are to renew our minds daily with the word of God and His plan for our life. We are not to think to highly of ourselves either, but in all things give the Lord the glory, for God has given all mankind a measure of faith and gifts that we will fulfill His purpose on the earth.

> For I say, through the grace given to me, to everyone, who is among you, not to <u>think</u> of himself more highly than he ought to <u>think</u>, but to <u>think</u> soberly, as God has dealt to each one a measure of faith. For as we have many members

in one body, but all the members do not have the same function. So we, being many, are one body in Christ, and individually members of one another. Having then gifts differing according to the grace that is given to us, let us prophesy in proportion to our faith; Or ministry, let us use it in our ministering; he who teaches, in teaching. He who exhorts, in exhortation; he who gives, with liberality; he who leads, with diligence; he who shows mercy, with cheerfulness. Let love be without hypocrisy. Abhor what is evil. Cling to what is good. be kindly affectionate to one another with brotherly love, in honor giving preference to one another. Not lagging in diligence, fervent in spirit, serving the Lord. Rejoicing in hope, patient in tribulation, continuing steadfastly in prayer. Distributing to the needs of the saints, given to hospitality. Bless those who persecute you; bless and do not curse. Rejoice with those who rejoice, and weep with those who weep. Be of the same mind toward one another. Do not set your <u>mind</u> on high things, but associate with the humble. Do not be wise in your own <u>opinion</u>. Repay no one evil for evil. Have regard for good things in the sight of all men. If it is possible, as much as depends on you, live peaceably with all men. Beloved, do not avenge yourselves, but rather give place to wrath; for it is written, "Vengeance is Mine, I will repay, says the Lord. Therefore "If your enemy is hungry, feed him; if he is thirsty, give him a drink; for in so doing you will heap coals of fire on his head. Do not be overcome by evil, but overcome evil with good. (Rom. 12:3–21)

> Finally, brethren, whatever things are true, whatever things are noble, whatever things are just, whatever things are pure, whatever things are lovely, whatever things are of good report, if there is any virtue and if there is anything praiseworthy—meditate (think) on these things. (Phil. 4:8)

This is what, we as children of God, are to think on and do. For in doing this, you will create the environment that God destined for you, which leads to increase in all things that pertain to your life here on earth. In our thought life, we should not think too highly of ourselves that pride comes in. On the other hand, do not think low of yourselves because we are seated high with our anointed king, Jesus

> Let this mind (thinking) be in you which was also in Christ Jesus. Who, being in the form of God did not consider it robbery to be equal with God? But made Himself of no reputation, taking the form of a bondservant, and coming in the likeness of men. And being found in appearance as a man. He humbled Himself and became obedient to the point of death, even the death of the cross. Therefore God also has highly exalted Him and given Him the name which is above every name, that at the name of Jesus every knee should bow, of those in heaven, and of those on earth, and of those under the earth. And that every tongue should confess that Jesus Christ is Lord, to the glory of God the Father. Therefore, my beloved, as you have always obeyed, not as in my presence only, but now much more in my absence, work out your own salvation with fear and trembling. For it is God who works in you both to will and to do for His good pleasure. Do all things without complaining and disputing.

That you may become blameless and harmless, children of God without fault in the midst of a crooked and perverse generation, among whom you shine as lights in the world. Holding fast the word of life, so that I may rejoice in the day of Christ that I have not run in vain or labored in vain. (Phil.2:5–16)

Our thinking should be in the will of God, and we do this by putting God first place in our lives. We must focus on living for Him, and in due time, we will be exalted (raised up). As when Adam was to cultivate the garden, we are to cultivate the garden (assignment). God has given us His Word, His thoughts, and how to put it to action. Adam and Eve chose in their actions to do the opposite of what God said to do and death fell on mankind. Now, it's up to you!" "Life and death are in the power of the tongue" (Prov. 18:21).

Creating Your Environment with what you do

The things that you do will either create a good environment or a bad one. We have talked about your actions in many incidences while speaking of your words and how you think. We just made the statement of Adam and Eve's actions in the Garden of Eden. Your actions are your choice. You may choose to do what you feel is right by God's standards, or choose to do what you feel is good to your flesh standards. The outcome, however, is accordingly to our actions.

For each one shall bear his own load. Let him who is taught the word share in all good things with him who teaches. Do not be deceived, God is not mocked; for whatever a man sows (does), that he will also reap. For he who sows to his flesh will of the flesh reap corruption, but he who sows to the Spirit will of the Spirit reap everlasting life. And let us not grow weary while doing well, for in due season we shall reap if we do not lose

heart. Therefore, as we have opportunity, let us
do good to all, especially to those who are of the
household of faith. (Gal. 6:5–10)

From the very beginning, when seedtime and harvest was established, whatever you sow, you would reap. But I thank our Heavenly Father (God) that He has mercy on us for while we were deep in sin. He forgave us and saved us. We do reap what we sow, but through the grace and mercy of God when we sow to the flesh, He doesn't hold all of it against us. Translated, we do not reap the full harvest of our fleshly seeds. Thank you, Lord Jesus.

> The Lord is merciful and gracious, Slow
> to anger, and abounding in mercy. He will not
> always strive with us, Nor will He keep His
> anger forever. He has not dealt with us according
> to our sins. Nor punished us according to our
> iniquities. For as the heavens are high above the
> earth. So great is His mercy toward those who
> fear Him. As far as the east is from the west, So
> far has He removed our transgressions from us.
> (Pss. 103:8–10)

Because of the grace and mercy of our Heavenly Father, we don't receive back all the negative things and sin we commit because of God's grace and mercy. On the other hand, He gives us abundantly more than what we ask for or think when we love Him and keep His commandments

> Now to Him who is able to do exceed-
> ingly abundantly above all that we ask or think,
> according to the power that works in us. To Him
> be glory in the church by Christ Jesus to all gen-
> erations, forever and ever, Amen. (Eph.3:20–21)

Now it shall come to pass, if you diligently obey the voice of the Lord your God, to observe carefully all His commandments which I command you today, and that the Lord your God will set you high above all nations of the earth. "And all these blessings shall come upon you and overtake you, because you obey the voice of the Lord your God: "Blessed shall you be in the city, and blessed shall you be in the country. "Blessed shall be the fruit of your body, the produce of your ground and the increase of your herds, the increase of your cattle and the offspring of our flocks. "Blessed shall be your basket and your kneading bowl. "Blessed shall you be when you come in, and blessed shall you when you go out. "The Lord will cause your enemies who rise against you to be defeated before your face; they shall come out against you one way and flee before you seven ways. "The Lord will command the blessing on you in your storehouses and in all to which you set your hand, and He will bless you in the land which the Lord your God is giving you. "The Lord will establish you as a holy people to Himself, just as He has sworn to you, if you keep the commandments of the Lord your God and walk in His ways. "Then all peoples of the earth shall see that you are called by the name of the Lord, and they shall be afraid of you." (Deut. 28:1–10)

The things that you do will affect what happens to you. If you serve the Lord by being *obedient*, you will have whatever you desire when you ask in the name of Jesus. The Word of God states that when you get what you ask, it glorifies Him. People will see the goodness of God on your life. It's God's good pleasure to supply all of your needs according to His riches in glory. He has given you everything you need that pertains to life and has given you specific guidelines (Holy Bible) to go by to see you prosper (increase) in all that you do.

Example: A woman stated that her life was in shambles. She was separated from her husband, living with another man, using drugs, her house had been foreclosed, depressed, and on top of everything else, her son was getting into all kinds of trouble and had recently been in police custody. Her son was still doing the same things and getting the same results. She was asked how does it make her feel that she had been telling her son to change his ways and do right knowing that he wouldn't get in to all the trouble that he was getting into if he would just have been obedient to her and the laws of the land. She replied she felt bad because her son was headed down the same road she went down. She went on to say, "I've seen that road and I'm just trying to help my son avoid some heartaches and setbacks". I reminded her that the Lord knows the beginning from the end. He sees all the heartaches we will encounter. The question was asked to her on what she thinks the Lord may feel about her hearing and knowing what to do about her life, but still doing the same old things and getting the same old results.

Parents would have all of their children to grow up, be in health, and have wonderful lives. They do their best to raise them right and instruct them on how to accomplish it. When the children disobey and find themselves in the wrong environment, they have no one to blame but themselves. Likewise, people of God, the Lord has given you all you need to have a productive life, and He keeps on instructing us through His word, the Holy Spirit, and the saints. The blame, if any, then falls on the individual. We can't blame our parents, our upbringing, or others because when we are born again—all things become new, and old things are passed away. 2 Corinthians 5:17 says, "Therefore, if anyone is in Christ, he is a new creation; old things have passed away; behold, all things have become new."

We no longer need to reflect on what happened in the past. Now, we have a heavenly Father who loves us, has blessed us, and has told us go and increase. Glory to God! We have a Father that is rich (created all things). He is creator of all things. He sees all things. He knows all things. Our Father is all powerful, all knowing, and there is no one greater on earth or in heaven. Our heritage is rich. No, it is royalty.

We are ambassadors (high ranking diplomatic reps) in this world, but not of this world. When we speak it, we are representing the kingdom of our Heavenly Father. When people see us, they should see the glory of our Father. When we go about our daily living, we do it with no worries because our heavenly Father is watching over us, and we know He won't put more on us then we may bare. Our Savior, the Lord Jesus, has all of the power in His hand, and He will do exceeding abundantly above all that we ask or even think. As children of the Most High God, we watch over our mouth, thoughts, and what we do because we know it's not about us, but about the family (body of believers) of our Heavenly Father. When one is down, we all are down. The Bible says the individual believers form a body with Christ Jesus being the Head of the Body.

> The God of our Lord Jesus Christ, the Father of glory, may give to you the spirit of wisdom and revelation in the knowledge of Him. The eyes of your understanding being enlightened; that you may know what is the hope of His calling, what are the riches of the glory of His inheritance in the saints. And what is the exceeding greatness of His power toward us who believe, according to the working of His mighty power. Which He worked in Christ when He raised Him from the dead and seated Him at His right hand in the heavenly places, Far above all principalities and power and might and dominion, and every name that is named, not only in this age but also in that which is to come. And He put all things under His feet, and gave Him to be head over all things to the church. Which is His body, the fullness of Him who fills all in all. and you He made alive, who were dead in trespasses and sins, In which you once walked according to the course of this

world, according to the prince of the power of the air, the spirit who now works in the sons of disobedience, Among whom also we all once conducted ourselves in the lusts of our flesh, ful-filling the desires of the flesh and of the mind, and were by nature children of wrath, just as the others. But God, who is rich in mercy, because of His great love with which He loved us, Even when we were dead in trespasses, made us alive together with Christ (by grace you have been saved). And raised us up together, and made us sit together in the heavenly places in Christ Jesus, That in the ages to come He might show the exceeding riches of His grace in His kindness toward us in Christ Jesus. For by grace you have been saved through faith, and that not of yourselves; it is the gift of God." (Eph. 1:20–22; 2:1–8)

In this passage from the book of Ephesians, the Apostle Paul, the writer through the Spirit of the Lord, is telling us who we are, where we came from, and where we are going. We did live according to our flesh (what made us feel good) at a time in our lives. Now, we live through the knowledge and wisdom of Christ Jesus our Lord and Savior. No longer do we not know our purpose in life, no longer do we do according to our flesh, and no longer will we allow the devil to steal our joy. We are children of the Most High God, and it is by His grace and our faith that we are children of our Heavenly Father. He loves you, and He said if you love Him, keep His commandments! Do these three things, watch your words, watch your thinking, and watch what you do. By doing these three things, you will create your godly environment.

How to Change Your Thinking, Your Words, and Your Actions

At this point you may be thinking it sounds good, but how may I change my thinking.

Keep in mind you change your thinking by focusing and thinking on what you desire things to be, and not on what you don't won't things to be in your life. Who you associate yourself with, and what you allow yourself to see and hear will determine what will be in your life. Your eyes and ears are soil for seed. Whatever you see or hear goes into your heart, and whatever goes in comes out. Because your ears keep taking it in at a point and time it will come out, unless you nurture (cultivate) your garden (heart) with words of faith or other godly substances (Holy Bible, attending a Church, Godly music, Godly programming), and whatever you spend the most time sowing (doing) is usually were your focus (thinking) will be. Remember, as a man thinks (what he thinks about), so will he be.

This is why you need to monitor who you associate yourselves with. If you are not ministering to a sinner or backslider and not working with them because you have no choice, then why are you around them? We must watch who we fellowship with. The Bible encourages you to have fellowship with other believers. Hebrews 10:24–25 says, "And let us consider one another in order to stir up love and good works. Not forsaking the assembling of ourselves together, as is the manner of some, but exhorting one another, and so much the more as you see the Day approaching."

Assembling together in church or a fellowship with believers is enriching to your soul (helps your emotions and feelings). People of like faith may encourage one another, lift one another up, and support one another. Church is more than a building, it's a body of believers that form a heavenly family down here on earth, with God the Creator as their Heavenly Father. There is a scripture in the Old Testament, "Iron sharpens iron, so a man sharpens the countenance of his friend" (Prov. 27:17). What that is referring to is if you both are iron, then your coming together will make you both sharper, but if one is iron and the other something else, the iron (Christian) will not get any sharper.

This will also strengthen you so when you are out in the world or ministering you will have fed your spirit man with the words of God and be well equipped to be led by the Spirit of God. In Luke 4:4, it says, "It is written, 'Man shall not live by bread alone, but by every word of God.'" For all of God's children "overcome the enemy by their testimonies (our words of faith, and what the Lord has done for us), the Blood of the Lamb (Jesus sacrifice for us), and we love not our lives unto the death" (Rev. 12:11).

> When He had called the people to Himself, with His disciples also, He said to them, "Whoever desires to come after Me, let him deny himself, and take up his cross, and follow Me. "For whoever desires to save his life will lose it, but whoever loses his life for my sake and the gospel's will save it. "For what will it profit a man if he gains the whole world, and loses his own soul? "Or what will a man give in exchange for his soul? "For whoever is ashamed of me and my words in this adulterous and sinful generation, of him the Son of Man also will be ashamed when He comes in the glory of His Father with the holy angels." (Mark 8:34–38)

There is no better way to live than for the One whom created you. We are saying the way to live out this life starts with your thinking on the ways of God. The Lord instructed Joshua exactly how to have good success.

> This book of the Law shall not depart from your mouth, but you shall meditate (thinking it over) in it day and night, that you may observe to do according to all that is written in it. For then you will make your way prosperous, and then you will have good success. "Have I not commanded you? Be strong and of good courage; do not be afraid, nor be dismayed, for the Lord your god is with you wherever you go." (Josh. 1:8–9)

When you meditate (think it over) on the word, you are sowing into your heart. Meditating on the Word of God sows into your heart seed that will produce a good harvest.

Once you understand this truth you will know the only way to have the life that our Creator God destined for us to have is to sow the word, speak the word, and do the word. The power is in your mouth to live or die. Confessing who you are and what you will accomplish is speaking into existence things that are not as though they were.

As my spiritual leader, Dr. Osborne Richards, says, "If you be honest with God, and do your best for Him, you will never be ashamed." It took me a while to fully understand those words. When you do these things, you are in a godly place no matter what is going on around you. When you are operating like this, you are confident that all things do work out for your good. So how in the world could I be ashamed when I know my God is watching over me?

If you choose to think on words in the Bible instead of what your problems may be, the outcome would be far better. Life is too short to allow the enemy to steal your joy. So if you decide that you want a peaceful environment, it's up to you to create it. For instance, "if you have anything in your heart against anyone, forgive them, that your Father in heaven may also forgive you your wrong doings" (Mark 11:25). Scripture also encourages one to have this mentality, "Or finally, brethren, whatever things are true (word of God), whatever things are noble, whatever things are just, whatever things are pure, whatever things are lovely, whatever things are of good report, if there is any virtue and if there is anything praiseworthy-meditate on these things" (Phil. 4:8). Make up in your mind that life is to short to waste it away being upset and depressed. The Bible encourage us that this life is not ours to own, and yes, we are to live an abundant life, but through the purpose of our Heavenly Creator God. We are living to use our gifts and talents, the Lord God has given us, and we are on assignment destined to increase in everything that we do;

God blessed them and told them to be fruitful, multiply, fill the earth, subdue it, and have dominion over it. (Gen. 1:28).

Example: A person has been diagnosed with cancer. She is a woman of faith and has prayed about it. Now, every day, she waters her words with faith. She knows that in the Holy Bible, it says, "Himself (Jesus) bore our sins in His own body on the tree, that we, having died to sins, might live for righteousness, by whose stripes you were healed" (1 Peter 2:24). This is a strong statement, for it is saying because of what Jesus did on Calvary, you are already healed. Now. all you need to do is to believe this word, speak this word, and wait on the manifestation (something revealed). St. James said it this way, "Is any sick among you? Let him call for the elders of the church, and let them pray over him, anointing him with oil in the name of the Lord (Jesus). The prayer of faith shall save the sick, and the Lord shall raise him up" (James 5:14). There are many scriptures in the Holy Bible speaking about healing. You read and think on Bible scriptures, relating to your needs, and you will reap what you have sown from the word of God.

Example: Your husband left you, the kids are in trouble with the law, and your job is going out of business. Many would say this lady is going through hell or she must be in a desperate state of mind. The Word of God lets us know that there is nothing to hard for God.

And we should "cast all of our cares upon Him for Him care for us." Again, we find in the word of God what we need to say, think, and do. Then and only then will you have the God kind of success (complete and whole), praise the Lord!

> Rejoice in the Lord always, Again I will say, rejoice! Let your gentleness be known to all men. The Lord is at hand. "Be anxious (Worry) for nothing, but in everything by prayer and supplication, with thanksgiving, let your requests be made known to God. And the peace of God, which surpasses all understanding, will guard your hearts and minds through Christ Jesus. Finally, brethren, whatever things are true, whatever things are noble, whatever things are just, whatever things are pure, whatever things are lovely, whatever things are of good report, if there is any virtue and if there is anything praiseworthy, meditate on these things. (Phil. 4:4–7)

> "Is anything too hard for the Lord? (Gen. 18: 14)

God did not intend for man to increase in unrighteousness, nor to be sick, and definitely not to be alone, or anything outside of being blessed and increasing (Gen. 1:28). Because of the choice to allow one's thinking to be on worldly things, we miss the mark of our high calling. As in Adam and Eve surrendering to worldly needs, Jesus came to renew our thinking so that we would see ourselves as God sees us and who we were created to be. His children created in His own image and to be complete, spirit, soul, and body after His likeness. Because of Adam and Eve's sin, in order to get back to the plan of God, we must be born again, for every one that is born again is a child of the Most High God.

It is not too late to renew your mind and to obey the Father as He instructed Joshua.

Our Heavenly Father loves you so much He didn't leave you in that fallen state but sent His only begotten Son (Jesus) to redeem you back to Himself. In doing so, He put us back into His presence to fulfill our God-given destined—to increase, increase, and increase. And this is to increase and multiply after His kind, not the devil's kind, for we are children of righteousness. Now, when we look at that verse, which says, "What is man that you are mindful of him, or the son of man that you take care of him (Heb. 2:6)? Even the angels see that you have the favor of God.

We (you) are destined to be royal agents for the kingdom, prospering in everything you touch for the glory of the Father. When people see you, they should see a representation (His image and His Likeness) of the living God, Jesus the Christ in you. We must think in line with our savior.

> Let nothing be done through selfish ambition or conceit, but in lowliness of mind let each esteem others better than himself. Let each of you look out not only for his own interests, but also for the interests of others. Let this mind be in you, which was also in Christ Jesus. (Phil. 2:3–5)

The word of God instructs the believer to have a mind like the Savior, God's only begotten Son, Jesus "who humbled Himself and became obedient unto death and was highly exalted."

> Who being in the form of God did not consider it robbery to be equal with God? But made Himself of no reputation, taking the form of a bondservant, and coming in the likeness of men. And being found in appearance as a man, He humbled Himself and became obedient to the point of death, even the death of the cross. Therefore God also has highly exalted Him and given Him the Name which is above every name" (Jesus). (Phil. 2:6–9)

Your Destiny Revealed

The Lord Jesus has given us the example of living for the Father, dying to self. Then will your true destiny in this life be revealed? Keep in mind your destiny was revealed again in the New Testament. Jesus said, "I have come that you might have life and that you might have it more abundantly" (John 10:10).

Get up out of that worldly thinking and renew your mind to who you are (a child of God), know who your father (God) is, and what you were destined to be (blessed and highly favored to increase). When you are increasing, the kingdom of God is increasing.

"And whatever you ask in My name, that I will do, that the Father may be glorified in the Son" (John 14:13). The Lord Jesus gave examples on what the kingdom of heaven was like, found in the book of Matthew.

> "For the kingdom of heaven is like a man traveling to a far country, who called his own servants and delivered his goods to them. "And to one he gave five talents, to another two, and to another one, to each according to his own ability; and immediately he went on a journey. "Then he who had received the five talents went and traded with them, and made another five talents. "And likewise he who had received two gained two more also. "But he who had received one went and dug in the ground, and hid his lord's money. "After a long time the lord of those servants came

and settled accounts with them "So he who had received five talents came and brought five other talents, saying, 'Lord, you delivered to me five talents; look, I have gained five more talents besides the.' "His lord said to him, 'Well done, good and faithful servant; you were faithful over a few things, I will make you ruler over many things. Enter into the joy of your lord.' "He also who had receive two talents came and said, 'Lord, you delivered to me two talents; look, I have gained two more talents besides them.' "His lord said to him, 'Well done, good and faithful servant; you have been faithful over a few things, I will make you ruler over many things. Enter into the joy of your lord.' "Then he who had received the one talent came and said, 'Lord, I knew you to be a hard man, reaping where you have not sown, and gathering where you have not scattered seed. 'And I was afraid, and went and hid your talent in the ground. Look, there you have what is yours. "But his lord answered and said to him. 'You wicked and lazy servant, you knew that I reap where I have not sown, and gather where I have not scattered seed. 'So you ought to have deposited my money with the bankers, and at my coming I would have received back my own with interest... 'Therefore take the talent from him, and give it to him who has ten talents. 'For to everyone who has, more will be given and he will have abundance; but from him who does not have, even what he has will be taken away. (Matt. 25:14–29)

Do not let your talents go to waste, increase what God has given you. You were destined to increase in the name of the Lord Jesus Christ! The Lord showed me in His word that He is the only Living

God, ever increasing, and His kingdom is ever increasing through His Children.

As children of the Most High God, we must renew our thinking to the fact that He is able and willing to supply all of our needs according to His Riches. If God's children would realize that they have a Heavenly Father, who sits high and looks low and has all power in His hands, they would understand they win. When He speaks a thing, it will come to pass. Whatever He has said about you in His word, it's true. God the Father goes on to say, "No weapon form against you shall prosper" (Isa. 54:17a). In other words, nothing may come against you that will overtake you, for the Most High Powerful, loving God, will Keep you in His peace and protection. You are blessed and highly favored by the only Creator God!

Who also say in His Holy Word (Bible), 'it is written: "Eye has not seen, nor ear heard. Nor have entered into the heart of man the things which God has prepared for those who love Him. But God has revealed them to us through His Spirit. For the Spirit searches all things, yes, the deep things of God. For what man knows the things of a man except the spirit of the man which is in him? Even so no one knows the things of God except the Spirit of God. Now we have received, not the spirit of the world, but the Spirit who is from God, that we might know the things that have been freely given to us by God (1 Cor 2:9-12).

Remember, God has a plan for you and the cares of this life have no power over a child of God. You are in the world, but not of this world. You will resist the trials and temptation of this world and sow the Word of God, thinking the best is yet to come in God, and doing your best, living your best by faith in the Name of your Lord and Savior, Jesus the Christ. Amen. Glory to God.

You were destined to increase!

A Special thank you, to my son Darrow Jr., my sister's Latrice Winn, Regina Wilson, and Zenada Greer for your support and encouragement. Also, I recognize my beautiful children, Jerome, Raegan, Daniel, Moriah, John and my loving parents, Clarence and Willa Winn. Love you Family!

Your brother in Christ the Lord,
Evangelist Pastor: Darrow Smith
P.O. Box 18093
Cincinnati, OH 45218

About the Author

Darrow Smith has served faithfully in ministry since 2000. He is a family man, a father of six, and a grandfather of five grandchildren.

Darrow Smith is called into the ministry to serve, preach, teach, and encourage others—his greatest gift being encouragement. He is a native of Lexington, Kentucky, and now resides in Cincinnati, Ohio. He attended Rhea Bible Institute in Broken Arrow, Oklahoma, and has received a master's degree in biblical theology and a bachelor's degree in business management from Cincinnati Christian University.

Evangelist Smith has served as a pastor for twelve years. For nine years, he serves as senior pastor of Changing Lives Ministries Int'l where he also serves as an outreach evangelist, spreading the good News of our Lord Jesus the Christ with the special calling to unify the body of Christ, with a focus on believers' inheritance as a child of God and the authority that comes with being a child of God.

Being divinely called to Changing Lives Ministries, at a time such as this, Evangelist Darrow displays a genuine love for all people. He is truly a servant of God who has well equipped him to walk into This calling.

CPSIA information can be obtained
at www.ICGtesting.com
Printed in the USA
LVHW091108031120
670569LV00004B/514

9 781098 016913